Just Wobbling Along

My first five years with Parkinson's Disease

Helga Mellor Macfarlane

DEDICATION

To My Parents, Roy & Helene
-   Whose love, values, and quest for knowledge laid the solid foundation on which I now so rely. I am thankful they will never see in person this journey I find myself on for it would have broken their hearts, but I know they are guiding me.

And to My Son, Murray
-   The light of my life, my reason for being, my purpose, my future, my whole heart, my everything.

Table of Contents

ACKNOWLEDGMENTS

First and foremost, I must pay tribute to every single scientist who devotes their working career to developing drugs and treatments that cure or reduce the suffering of those with any kind of illness or disability. They are the world's unsung heroes.

I cherish our NHS and its staff and hope against all hope that in years to come this incredible institution and the vast array of people at all levels that work in it are given the support and value they deserve. But all credit must also be given to the many dedicated health-related professionals who work outside the NHS privately, and also those teaching our up and coming generations.

Me though? I would be nothing without my family and close friends - the people who loyally stick by me day-in day-out, through all the ups and downs of life. I hope I give you as much as you give me.

These are the people closest to my heart:

John & Murray, my husband and son - you do more for me than you will ever know. I am a Mellor and I am a Macfarlane - family is everything.

My lifelong special pal Mainzer, for always being there, and who endured proof-reading this book.
Moira, the teacher who fired my love for music and gives me laughs and support every day.
Richard, who has endlessly helped and stood by me, and his family for welcoming and supporting me like one of their own.

Brian, Josie, and Lindsay T, who have shone through as true friends.

Sarah and Bruce, the world's best physios - they are my absolute saviours in so many ways. You both have my utmost respect and thanks.

Much credit to Gordon W, the childhood friend and neighbour whom I linked up with again after nearly forty years, and who was the catalyst for me writing this book. Without his patience, help, and advice I would have never had the courage to do it.

And our adorable cats Muzz and Lizzie, who did their best to hinder me by standing on my laptop and constantly distracting me.

1. ONE FINE DAY

Monday 10th August 2015

Well, that day didn't quite turn out as planned! It was a beautiful sunny Monday, the last of the school summer holidays, and I had taken the day off work to go cycling in a nearby forest with my 15 year-old son. We loaded the bikes on to the car and off we went, me glowing inside at the thought of special mum/son time with my fast growing-up boy. We off-loaded at the other end, got togged up, and set off. It had been raining overnight and the air smelt beautifully fresh and wholesome as the forest floor and majestic Scots Pines dried off.

The track was rutted from a summer's worth of cyclists and walkers and was still a bit muddy as we slowly negotiated the narrow entrance gate. I felt the front wheel of my bike slip a bit and put my right foot down to steady myself - SNAP! The sound ricocheted around the open space and a searing pain shot up my leg - I knew immediately that I had broken my ankle. We had gone less than twenty feet from the car - what an epic fail.

Not that that wasn't bad enough on its own, but little did I know that it would mark the start of a life-long mystery journey.

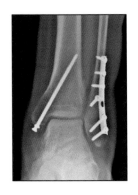

I had my ankle re-built with an assortment of screws and metal plates, it was plastered up and so began the road to recovery. Six weeks in plaster with crutches and no weight-bearing, six weeks without plaster, different crutches, and gradual weight-bearing, then lots of physiotherapy.

'In six months you'll be right as rain', the orthopaedic surgeon told me, 'and if you do your exercises, there's no reason why you won't be able to run again.'

Running was one of my passions, so I was determined to be good, do as I was told and hopefully hit the roads again by the following Easter, if not next Summer at the latest.

There wasn't much I could do at first all plastered up, but they'd said to regularly waggle my toes to keep the circulation going, relieve the swelling, avoid blood clots and maintain the muscle strength - so I waggled! But waggling wasn't quite as easy as I thought it would be. Sometimes my toes didn't want to waggle, or they'd go waggle-wild and start wobbling uncontrollably. As time went on the random waggle seemed to be spreading up my leg and my whole right side would start wobbling.

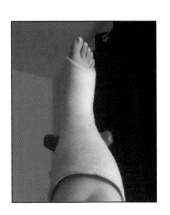

I mentioned it at my follow-up appointment, but was told it was simply because the nerves had been badly damaged and it would take some time to get the control back. That made sense.

The plaster came off - it had been a long six weeks and it felt like there were going to be mushrooms growing under it - there weren't but suffice to say it wasn't a pretty sight! It was fabulous to have a 'free' leg again although it did feel like I had a couple of elastic bands wrapped tightly around my ankle. The removal of the plaster meant my physiotherapy could start and I was well ready for it, desperate to get moving again.

Off I hurpled excitedly for my first session with my two different sized trainers on - a normal size 4 on my left foot and a size 6 on my still puffy right foot! It's amazing what you can get on eBay. I always wondered who was wearing the opposite lopsided set!

I got a whole four physiotherapy sessions from the NHS at my local hospital. Now, I worship the UK's National Health Service, we are so very lucky to have it, and rightly-so it is the envy of the world. But nothing is perfect, and this was one of the occasions that it wasn't.

The first session involved a newly qualified physiotherapist being overseen by his boss. The poor lad was utterly terrified - he stuttered and stumbled as she fired questions at him, and every time he touched my ankle his face went an even brighter shade of red than his bright red hair. I spent the whole forty minutes so intent on putting on my most encouraging face and willing him to survive the ordeal that I couldn't bring myself to mention the weird lack of control I felt in my foot and ankle.

Thankfully at the following session he was alone, but he'd had the stuffing knocked out of him so much he started every sentence with 'Sorry'. Once again, I hadn't the heart to mention my wonky waggly foot.

At session three I learned that my poor ginger friend, whom I actually thought had the makings of a very good physio with a lot of empathy, had been moved to another small hospital up north and had been replaced by what transpired to be his polar opposite. This guy proudly informed me he was no novice like his predecessor and had been in the job for a year. Well, bully for him I thought as he marched around like he owned the place. Grrrrr!

He immediately took my crutches from me and ordered 'Walk!'.

I did a few laps back and forth at varying speeds as instructed as he watched. It really hurt.

Then he said, 'Now I want you to hop.'

I looked at him with utter incredulity. 'Sorry?' I said, with visions flashing through my mind of bent metal and splintered bones. 'Are you sure? It's really painful just walking...' I muttered.

'Oh yes. Got to get those muscles strengthened up.' he pronounced.

I hesitatingly tried. It was almost impossible and apart from being insanely painful it just felt so wrong. He could clearly see I was struggling so conceded that I could practice it at home on a soft carpet holding on to the wall if I really had to. So I did, and it was awful. I was all over the place like a drunken one-legged kangaroo - but who am I to argue with professional opinion?

I was angry with him when I went to see him a fortnight later. My ankle was sorer than it had been and I felt I had lost some control of it rather than gained any.

This time he had me walking up and down the stairs. Down was extremely difficult when my injured ankle had to bend as I moved the other foot from the step above to the step below.

'Bend it!' he kept shouting.

'I can't!' I'd retort, but he wasn't for believing me and kept just shouting 'Bend, bend, bend, bend …' on each step like an army major.

Exasperated, I finally stopped, took a deep breath and calmly said to him 'Look, I'm fifty-one years of age and it may surprise you to know that I *do* know how to walk downstairs. My ankle - will - not – bend. In fact, it doesn't really want to do anything I, you or anyone else wants it to do, and any amount of you shouting 'bend' is not going to change that.' My tone of voice was rising...

There was an awkward silence. I felt quite uncomfortable as answering back is not normal for me, but I felt upset, confused, and worried. Something about it all was bugging me but I didn't know what.

Mr. Super-Confident-Physio just looked at me and said, 'Okay, practice it at home then. I'm signing you off, you'll be fine.'

I left. I felt defeated. It was as though I had fallen at the very first hurdle, but more than anything I had this underlying uneasiness that things weren't going to go my way.

2. THE CONUNDRUM

I was 50 years-old and darned fit when I broke my ankle if I do say so myself! In my late 40's, I was running twelve to eighteen miles, three to four times a week and I loved it. However, I was starting to think that age was catching up a little with the arrival of the big 5-0 as my miles were dwindling slightly and I was finding it difficult to get into that rhythm that keeps runners pounding along eating the miles. I was somehow having to concentrate more. Every runner has good and bad spells, I was totally used to that so didn't think much of it. Indeed, I never really regarded myself as 'a runner' anyway, more just a person who likes running. I wasn't a natural distance runner by any stretch of the imagination, if anything sprinting was more my thing, but it was the fresh air, the freedom, and the connection with nature that fuelled my addiction to running.

As time went on I was increasingly finding the wonderful sights, sounds, and smells of the outdoors were passing me by unnoticed as my mind seemed to have to focus harder on getting one foot to keep going in front of the other. Age, the onset of menopause, work stress, a phase, general stress, some other stress - I just couldn't put my finger on it but I was sure it would pass as just one of the usual ups and downs.

I was so scunnered (good Scottish word for fed-up) after my NHS physio experience that I had a few weeks of burying my head in the sand of work and hoping my foot and ankle would magically sort themselves out.

However, those who know me well will know that I'm a stubborn sod when I want to be, so I decided to consult a private physio recommended to me by various fit friends in the know about these things. I've always believed that nothing is more valuable than your health, so I was happy to spend some of my hard-earned cash on getting myself fixed.

He looked, he watched, he manipulated. I could see my new physio thinking and could almost hear the cogs of his brain, which clearly held vast knowledge, turning. He seemed to instinctively know what would work and what wouldn't, what would hurt and what wouldn't. I somehow knew I was on to a good thing with him. He sent me away with exercises that I could completely see the reasoning behind, and I worked my socks off on them for the following week's session.

Again, he looked, he watched, and he manipulated - all the time thinking, thinking, thinking. I loved it - it was fascinating watching him at work, an absolute master of his craft. I was learning lots too as he explained the workings of my foot and what seemed to be going wrong. To make things even better though, his academic prowess carried with it an utterly hilarious line of banter better than any comedian! He would have me laughing in mirth and crying in pain at the same time.

I did all the exercises he gave me as though my life depended on them. I just wanted to be made better. So much so, that I started noticing a slight tremor in my hand and joked with him that perhaps I'd been overdoing it a bit.

But as the appointments continued, he started frowning a little more each time until, after about the fourth or fifth appointment, he said, 'This just isn't fixing properly. I've seen plenty of broken ankles and something just isn't right. It's simply not responding the way it should. I think you need to go and see your doctor - tell him what I've said.'

Oh. I knew that if he said something wasn't right, then it definitely wasn't right.

Hats off to the GP, he was excellent! A quick examination and he agreed something did not seem quite right. There and then he picked up the phone and called the hospital to have my ankle looked at, and within four days I was back at the orthopaedic department. It was exactly one week short of six months since I'd had the accident. Unfortunately, I remember that for the wrong reason.

The consultant pondered over my notes then said gruffly 'Your GP should know better than to refer you back to me within six months.'

I sheepishly said, '...yes, that's next week.'

He stared straight at me, '...and next week is next week. So, I'd respectfully ask that you give it the correct amount of time and come back and see me after the *full* six months has elapsed if there's no improvement.'

I was gob-smacked. He had totally caught me off guard. I hurriedly started putting on my shoes and socks muttering 'Oh, right, yes... I'm sorry... er ... yes, thanks.'

I shot out of the room, grabbed my husband from the waiting room, dashed to the car and promptly dissolved in tears. Oh dear...

My physio was astonished and did a great job of pacifying me and reassuring me that we'd get to the bottom of it. I had total faith in him and so we worked on. Despite my strength getting better, we both knew I was struggling. I would do what he told me but could never control my foot and leg enough to sustain the repetitions the way I should have been able to - it was like my leg was receiving a bad Wi-Fi signal from my brain.

Once again, he urged me to go back to the GP, so I did.

It was a different GP this time, my usual lovely lady doctor, and she stopped me while I was telling her the reason for my visit and said 'Your lip is trembling while you're speaking, do you feel very nervous?.'

I said no, I was absolutely fine. However, I did mention that I was really struggling to sleep. She suggested that breaking my ankle so badly was perhaps a bigger trauma than I had realised and that could easily explain the trembling and poor sleep. She said she would like to try me on a course of anti-depressants. The appointment had gone in a completely different direction from the way I'd anticipated. I was certain I wasn't depressed but agreed to give them a go, even though in the back of my mind I knew I'd be back, and I was - they made not an iota of a difference. I appreciated her trying though.

At the next visit she did the whole follow my finger, touch your nose routine, etc. There was no denying I had a right handed tremor but she said it was most likely a harmless Essential Tremor, which can happen for no reason and can come and go. However, just to be on the safe side she made a referral for me to see a neurologist.

3. ANOTHER HITCH

The weeks went by while I waited for my appointment with the neurologist. Just to complicate matters, in the interim, I was diagnosed with the inherited heart condition Hypertrophic Cardiomyopathy and fitted with an implantable cardioverter defibrillator after repeated episodes of irregular heart rhythm and fainting - but at least it took my mind off the impending neurology visit.

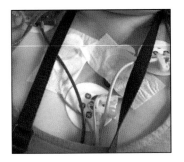

I was in hospital for more than a week with a spaghetti junction of wires attached to me. I remember being very self-conscious about my tremor - but strangely enough not one health professional questioned it. I didn't think anything of it at the time, but in hindsight, I find that quite surprising and a little concerning. I recall my dear Dad, when he was repeatedly in hospital with heart problems in his later years (yes, he seems to have passed on a little genetic gift to me!), saying he felt that many of the foreign doctors he came across seemed to have a more holistic approach compared to the UK ones and were more willing to look beyond the immediate problem in front of them. An interesting observation. Are our medics too blinkered in this country?

At last, it was neurology day! I normally go to hospital appointments on my own. Hospitals, medical procedures, blood, injections, incisions, operations, etc., none of it bothers me, but the fact that I brought my husband and even took him into the room with me (unheard of) when I was called, shows I was sub-consciously more concerned than I was letting on, even to myself.

The neurologist was a very quietly spoken man who seemed to have been blessed with only one facial expression and tone of voice, but that's by the by! He repeated all the nose touching and finger following things that the GP had done but was mysteriously doing them on my good arm? I eventually thought I ought to point this out. He nodded and said blandly 'Yes, I know.' Oops! Embarrassing! I shut up and decided to stick to doing what I was told.

Some further handholding and rather large arm-spiralling and he seemed satisfied. 'I am ninety-nine percent certain you have a thing called Functional Tremor, which can certainly be caused by a limb injury damaging the nerve circuitry.' he said, sounding like it was the most inconsequential thing ever.

His prognosis was that it may or may not get better, there was nothing he or I could really do to help it and there is no treatment. I felt somehow short-changed and made kind of grumbly 'is that it then' type noises. I think just to appease me he said he'd refer me for a precautionary brain scan purely to rule out anything sinister. However, he warned that I'd be low in the pecking order so not to expect it any time soon - but I was happy to just know it was coming.

I decided to put it to the back of my mind and get on with life. My handwriting was increasingly erratic which was becoming a problem at work, and the only way around this that I could see was to start teaching myself to write with my left hand. For a while, it was a toss-up between my script looking like that of a dottery 80 year-old if I used my right hand, or that of a clumsy 6 year-old if I used my left.

One day I suddenly found myself confronted with a rather important document to sign in front of a lawyer and realised I couldn't do it properly with either hand. It was excruciatingly embarrassing explaining the problem, although the lawyer calmly reassured me that there were 'options' if I found myself unable to write. I was horrified - potentially the rest of my life having to say to people 'I'm sorry, I can't write - could you write it for me?' Absolutely no way was I going to live my life like that. No. No. No!

I went home and night after night I covered pages and pages of a notebook replicating my signature and writing anything and everything, whatever came into my head, with my left hand.

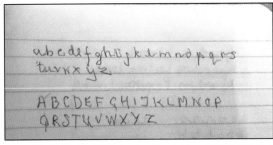

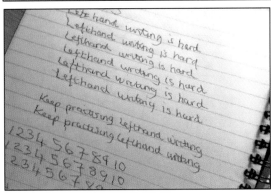

Very slowly it got better, especially in uppercase, and gradually my left hand signature started to resemble my right hand one. Although my left handed efforts were little by little becoming more acceptable to the eye, I was still very slow so taking phone messages at work was impossible. I devised a system of using the voice recorder on my phone. I would repeat everything back to the caller saying out loud, 'Yes, Joe Blogs from Smith Limited. Telephone 01234 567890. Okay, you want to move tomorrow's meeting from 2 to 3pm.' Then I'd hang up and play it back bit by bit to give myself time to write it down.

One of my colleagues was particularly understanding and would do things like fill in forms for me as far as he could, without having to be asked, before passing them through to me to complete or sign. Bless him! He'd pull my leg about my wobbly writing accusing me of having had a bottle of vodka for my breakfast again, and I found making light of my situation was my best coping strategy. It was hard though, constantly finding ways around doing things that used to come naturally, and I was whacked at the end of every day.

The other thing about losing your natural ability to write, is that however hard I practiced, I knew my left handed efforts would never look the same as the way my right handed script had. I think your handwriting can often be a great reflection of your personality, and mine no longer was. I felt I had lost a bit of 'me'.

Out of work new problems were gradually starting to manifest themselves too. I was still trying but failing to get my running back together so thought I'd build up to it by walking. But there was something going wrong - it didn't feel right and I couldn't figure out why. I would come home from a walk with my back and shoulders killing me, and also sometimes horribly light-headed. What on earth was going on? I tried to concentrate on my posture - perhaps I was slouching - but that didn't work. It was only when I went out one day carrying a bag in my right hand that I realised. Strangely my right hand just wanted to be in my pocket, it didn't want to do the normal arm swinging thing at all. If I made it carry the bag it was uncomfortable and I quickly got sore.

I didn't like what was happening to me one bit. None of it made any sense. All I'd done was break my ankle - lots of people do that and bounce back to normal in no time, so why wasn't I? It started eating at me, was I being a drama queen or a complete hypochondriac? My confidence started slipping, my anxiety was rising, and I didn't know which way to turn.

4. THE CRUMBLE

I am blessed to have never suffered from mental health issues in my life, so it was a huge shock when the anxiety I'd been getting ripples of, suddenly engulfed me, body and mind. It took over my whole being virtually overnight and I became a different person, petrified of the world. There was nothing I could do and nowhere I could go to escape its evil grip controlling me. I knew it was irrational, but I was powerless to shake it off. I had to get help and I could tell the GP I'd known for many years was shocked when she saw me. I was literally begging her to take this monster from me, I pleaded with her to send me to a psychiatrist 'I'm going mad.' I sobbed. She did.

I was sent to the local psychiatric hospital for my first appointment. I was deeply disappointed in myself to find that I was worried someone recognised me there. I know plenty of people who have in the past or are now suffering from mental health issues, and I wish nothing but better times ahead for them. I certainly do not think any less of them. But clearly there is a stigma at the back of my mind somewhere that I didn't know I harboured. I was extremely angry with myself for that and gave myself a good talking to.

The consultant psychiatrist was a lovely soft-spoken, quite young, Irish lady. She didn't really do anything the GP had not, just gently talked and asked questions. However, I had been told she had greater prescribing powers than the doctor so I was glad to see her. I also figured she must have seen far worse than me so if she could fix them, surely she could fix me.

At the end of the appointment, she gave me my prescription and simply said, 'We'll get you right, don't worry.'

I wanted to, but I couldn't fully believe her, it seemed an impossible mountain to climb. However, it did give me a glimmer of hope that this nightmare would end. I clung on to her words.

I was diagnosed with PTSD, Post Traumatic Stress Disorder, as a result of the hideous succession of serious health issues that had landed on me within six months of each other. I was given a prescription for three different kinds of anti-depressant and anti-anxiety medication, all at their maximum doses. The first few weeks were a living hell, for me and equally as much for my husband. His patience and understanding were endless. I'd wake up in the night petrified for no reason and I'd have spells when I couldn't sit still or couldn't eat. I was frightened to be on my own and frightened to go out. The strange and surprising thing was that I was still completely rational in all my other thinking and if anyone had phoned me they wouldn't have known there was anything wrong. I just could not rationalise the anxiety. I couldn't talk myself out of it and that total lack of control over my own body and mind was absolutely terrifying.

Very gradually over the following weeks, the drugs started to do their job. The vice that was clamping my head and tormenting me started to come off and the blinkers shutting out the real world from my view began to widen.

As a result, my second appointment with the nice psychiatrist was far less of a blur - and she was just that, a nice lady. It amused me a little that she was actually quite scatty! She took wild notes in huge handwriting then would promptly lose her pen for the umpteenth time! She was clearly hugely over-worked but took it in good humour. At the end of the session, she took out her tattered diary to book me in for next time. As she flicked through the pages I could see that every single one was jam-packed with appointments, meetings, and scribbled reminders. With a schedule like that she should have been suffering the anxiety attacks not me!

Eventually, in her pleasant Irish lilt, she said 'Ach, I've got a minute for my lunch here, I'll just put you in there. You won't be minding me eating my sandwich will you?'.

I saw her twice more. The final time I walked in, make-up on and head held high, far more like my normal self although still heavily drugged, she clasped her hands in glee and excitedly said 'Well there you go, will you be looking at that! You've done a grand job!'.

She made me feel great! It was like she'd handed me a huge box of gift-wrapped confidence. I was sad to say goodbye to her. 'Thank you' wasn't nearly enough. She had given me my life back.

It bothered me though that I was still being propped up by popping a pharmacy's worth of pills every day. I made it my mission to change that, but I knew I had to tread extremely carefully so I didn't slide down the evil snake back to the start. No way did I ever want to go through that living hell again. So little bit by little bit, half a tablet at a time, over many months I very gradually cut down, all the time keeping completely alert to my state of mind. Reaching zero was a long journey but I eventually made it and was medication free again.

I have often heard it said that a recovered alcoholic is still an alcoholic but one who doesn't drink anymore - and you are only one drink away from being an alcoholic again. After that experience, I view anxiety similarly. Now that I have had it once it is always there in the back of my mind. I don't ever want to go there again so I am always trying to be aware of my stress levels so they don't tip me back into the anxiety abyss. I wouldn't wish it on my worst enemy. If you have never suffered from it, believe me, you are the lucky one. It is unimaginably awful.

Writing this chapter has been more difficult than I can describe. I have deep scars within from this episode of my life. They are well buried but putting it all down on paper has been a stark reminder that they are still there.

5. THE 'A' TEAM

It had now been more than a year since I had broken my ankle and the very first little tremors had begun. I was waiting for the brain scan and otherwise just carrying on with life as normal but with this infernal tremor. I was still trying to get back into running but it still wasn't working, so I was putting on weight which annoyed me. All was not rosy, but I kept telling myself it could be a whole lot worse.

My marvellous musculoskeletal physiotherapist was still putting up with me, working at getting the flexibility back into the badly damaged ligaments along the front of my ankle and also loosening off the aches and pains caused by tensing my muscles trying to control my tremoring right arm. He made no bones about it - I was a complete conundrum!

He'd greet me with 'Oh no, here she comes! What on earth have you got for me this week?' I was definitely a challenge to which he was determined to rise, and I enjoyed watching him trying to work me out!

'Now, if I do this, I would normally expect this to happen.' he'd explain as he demonstrated on my good side. 'But if I do the same on the other side... hmmm... what? Seriously? You're weird!'.

We'd laugh over and over, but we also both knew it wasn't right. He decided it was time to bring in reinforcements in the form of his neurological specialist physiotherapy colleague.

They decided my first session should be a dual one and it turned out to be one of the most interesting ninety minutes I have spent in my life. I felt so incredibly lucky to have found two such dedicated and knowledgeable people, and that they were prepared to take on my weird wobbliness.

Together they worked their way around my entire body, exchanging views, exploring options, pinpointing weaknesses, and paving a way forward. At the end, Mr. Musculoskeletal handed me over to Mrs. Neurological to take over my care on the promise that he was there whenever needed. I was so sad to see him go, but I knew that I had been passed into excellent hands.

The neuro physio sessions were quite different from the MSK ones, but I lapped them up! In the MSK ones I'd spend a lot of my forty-minute appointment lying back while Mr. MSK did all the work smoothing out my aches and pains with his magical medicinal hands. Admittedly he also possessed a talent for having me writhing in pain and he'd chirp gleefully 'No pain, no gain!', but in general it was a relaxing experience.

The neuro physio was all about finding my weaknesses and wonky bits and getting them working correctly. It was an hour of intense concentration for me, each time learning about my body, what it should and shouldn't do, and why. I soon discovered how much of some limb functions I had already unwittingly lost. I got the feeling that whatever transpired to be wrong with me, my neuro physio was going to be one of the most important people in my life from now on. For the first time I didn't feel utterly alone with what was happening to me.

I have met a good few health professionals in my time but my neuro physio outstrips pretty well all of them with her remarkable listening skills and tremendous empathy. From the start, she looked at the bigger picture like no other and focused on me as an individual like no other. It is so hard watching your body change and there aren't enough words to express how much difference it makes to have someone like this - a rock by my side, constantly assessing and guiding me with her enormous knowledge and wonderful humour. I value her opinion more than she can know and trust her advice implicitly.

Although I had the neurologist's assurance that he was ninety-nine percent certain I had Functional Tremor it didn't really sit right with me. There were too many other little physical annoyances that I couldn't put my finger on, and it was at a music rehearsal that alarm bells really started to ring.

Playing keyboards and trumpet were my other passions apart from running, and I was pretty proficient at both having studied Music at University. Halfway through our Sunday morning rehearsal, we dug out a piece we hadn't played for a while. The keyboard part had a series of fast repeated chords in the right hand and I suddenly realised I just couldn't do them anymore. I hadn't given them a second thought the last time we had played it, but now, however hard I tried, my right wrist just seized up and I had no control over it. Full-on fear washed over me. I couldn't wait to get home and start Googling Motor Neurone Disease, Brain Tumours, etc. I was seriously scared.

After doing some online research, although I couldn't exactly match my symptoms to those of any particular 'nasty' I read about, from that moment on I was certain it was something more sinister than Functional Tremor. Not having what I felt was an accurate diagnosis was now really starting to eat at me.

One morning I remembered on the way to work that we needed milk for our office, so I stopped at a rather dodgy shop on the way there. You know the kind - wire protecting the windows, security tags on the coffee jars, and a queue of worthies desperate to buy their breakfast in the form of a cheap two litre plastic bottle of cider. I got to the front of the sizeable queue and went into my purse to get some coins to pay. At that moment my tremor decided to rear its ugly head with a vengeance and coins flew everywhere from my uncontrollable fingers. I was apologising profusely, groveling around trying to pick them up with the whole queue impatiently watching me and absolutely nobody attempting to help me. I glanced up and saw the shop assistant standing with her arms crossed, chewing gum, shaking her head at me with a look of utter disgust on her face - she clearly thought I was some kind of drunk with alcoholic withdrawal jitters. She had probably seen plenty of them in that particular shop, but I was certainly not one! I felt insulted, dirty, and embarrassed. I wanted to scream at the entire shop 'For God's sake I've got xxxxx!' but I couldn't because I didn't know what xxxxx was.

6. THE TURNING POINT

Early in 2017 the appointment for my long-awaited brain scan finally dropped through the door. The letter arrived accompanied by an information leaflet telling me all about the special kind of scan I was to be getting - a DaTSCAN. Also enclosed was a packet of tablets to take for a couple days leading up to it, which apparently block the thyroid from getting unnecessary radiation. The whole thing was going to take the best part of a day. It sounded pretty serious stuff but I was ready for it - bring it on, at last!

DaTSCANs apparently detect the dopamine transporters in your brain, although there was no explanation in the leaflet as to why they were looking for them or what they did, and I subconsciously decided to remain in blissful ignorance. I could have Googled it, but I think there was some denial going on - if I didn't know, I wouldn't have whatever it was they were looking for. Stupid really, but a bit of self-preservation kicking in.

On the day, I reported in and was given an injection of a radioactive isotope that was going to show up these mystery dopamine receptor things, I then had a three-hour wait to give it time to find my brain!

Now, there's a particularly good café at our local hospital, not the one for the general public but one that staff use, that's tucked away up a back stairway. I knew about it thanks to a tip-off from a nurse when one or other of my elderly parents was in hospital some years earlier. Normally I'd have gone and revelled in filling my tummy with much tastiness there but tragically eating wasn't allowed before the procedure. So unfair! I guess they didn't want to risk anyone's dinner coming up in their valuable scanning machine. So, I opted for my second favourite occupation, napping, and went and had forty-plus winks in the car.

The scan itself was the most relaxing hour of peace and quiet I'd had in a long time, helped along by a radiographer with a voice so soothing she could have hypnotised me into parting with my life savings!

In fact, the most difficult parts of the day transpired to be finding a parking space and filling in the various consent forms legibly with my newly trained left hand, with a nurse hanging over me watching. At the end, they told me I looked so comfortable on the scanner they'd thrown in a bonus CT scan too. Bingo - the more investigations the better!

All the same, I went home glad it was over. Although I was deeply concerned about what was happening to my body, I do tend to have a positive outlook on life and I suppose a bit of the 'It'll never happen to me' thing we all do, so I never really gave it too much thought after that. La la la... it'll be fine... Life was busy anyway with a big job and a family to run, so I didn't have too much time to dwell.

Three weeks after the brain scan an appointment with the consultant neurologist arrived. Now call me pessimistic but I was fairly sure our overstretched NHS wouldn't waste a valuable appointment for him to just say it's all fine and send me on my merry way. Hmmm... I purposefully parked that thought to the back of my mind.

My appointment was at 12 o'clock on Thursday 27th April 2017.

I went to work first which was a bit pointless as I didn't achieve very much other than watching the clock all morning. Needless to say, we set off far too early for the appointment, despite my long-suffering husband telling me repeatedly we were far too early - it's a really annoying habit of mine! I'd save myself so much stress in life if I didn't do that whenever I have something important on. I end up sitting twiddling my thumbs making myself twice as nervous as I would have been if I had got there at a sensible time. Added to that Sod's Law dictates that the higher your level of tension the later the appointment will be running. The neurologist was running twenty minutes late, which despite my husband's best efforts to distract me, gave me loads of time to read all the posters on the walls of the waiting room advertising support groups, disability services, hospice care, etc. Not what I needed to see.

At last, the neurologist called me through and sat me down.

'How are you?' he said matter-of-factly.

'I'm fine thanks!' I chirped - kind of my stock answer whenever anybody asks me that.

'Have you got anyone with you?' he asked, so I told him my husband was in the waiting room.

'I'll go and get him.' he replied making for the door.

Thud - a lump landed in my stomach. I immediately knew the news wasn't going to be good and I could tell by my husband's face when he came in, he was thinking exactly the same thing.

Wasting no time and without a hint of emotion whatsoever the neurologist pointed to the scan picture on his computer screen. In an unnervingly quiet voice, he said, 'Do you see that bright area on the left there - well it's much bigger than the corresponding area on the other side of your brain. That is absolutely typical of Parkinson's Disease. You have Parkinson's Disease.'

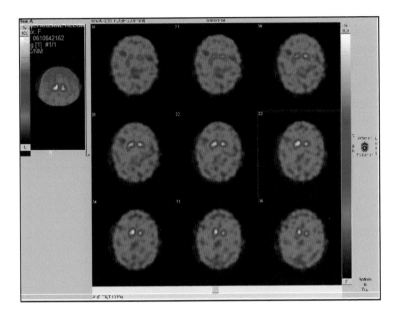

Talk about hitting me with it straight on, no messing.

Pause. Silence.

I sighed, smiled resignedly, and said in a somewhat robotic fashion 'Oh, right... well ... thank you for doing the scan.'

He looked at me rather oddly for a good few seconds and said in his usual monotone 'You are taking this very well?'.

I'm not sure whether he thought I hadn't understood what he'd said, was in complete denial, or was perhaps expecting me to throw myself on the floor kicking and screaming. In actual fact, my first and foremost emotion was huge relief. I was relieved that at long last I knew what I was dealing with so could finally move forward appropriately and do exactly that, deal with it.

I replied 'To be honest I thought I had something like that, and you haven't told me I have a Brain Tumour and you haven't told me I have Motor Neurone Disease, so I guess it could be far worse.' (Don't anyone try to tell me these things don't cross your mind when weird things start happening to your movement and coordination).

'Is there anything you want to ask?' he offered more out of duty than compassion. Of course, there were a million things I wanted to ask but right at that moment I couldn't think of a single one of them.

'So, what now?' was the best I could do.

'Well, nothing really.' he replied, 'We'll just wait and see how you get on. I'll ask one of our specialist Parkinson's nurses to make contact with you, and I'll see you again in a year.' he concluded in a 'time-up' kind of voice, closing my notes. And that was it.

The whole thing took fifteen minutes.

Fifteen minutes to change the entire course of my future. I had officially embarked upon an unexpected mystery tour into the unknown world of Parkinson's Disease, that would map the rest of my life.

7. THE NEW ROAD

I don't really remember the walk back to the car, but I do remember thinking I should be upset, but I wasn't. The feeling that was emerging as I took each step more solidly than the last was resigned determination.

We got into the car and I said in answer to my husband's inevitable question as to how I was feeling. 'It is what it is, I just have to deal with it. I have to not let it beat me.'

We went back to work. I mean, seriously - who on earth goes back to work after getting a diagnosis of Parkinson's Disease? But it seemed the 'normal' thing to do and I felt that it was more important than ever right now to preserve 'normal'. Normal, normal, normal. Suddenly that word had taken on a new so much more precious meaning. I was still the same normal person who had left work an hour earlier so I was surely still the same normal person coming back?

My closest work colleague was at his desk working away 'normally' when I reached the office. He looked up and said casually as though I'd just popped out to the shop, 'How did you get on?'.

'I've got Parkinson's Disease.' I replied.

He paused, then strung together the longest line of expletives I have ever heard! It was utterly hilarious and we both ended up in fits of laughter - exactly what I needed.

Needless to say, being at work that afternoon was a complete waste of time and after a couple of hours of robotically performing tasks but not really achieving anything I decided to call it a day and head home. I really did need to gather my thoughts.

I have to admit to feeling a bit peeved. I already had a serious genetic heart defect that necessitated an implantable cardioverter defibrillator and now Parkinson's Disease. Wasn't that a bit unfair - wouldn't it have been more decent to share things out a bit better rather than dump them both on me?

I quickly came to the conclusion that I had two choices moving forward – to make the lives of me and everyone around me a misery by letting it drag me down or to do everything I could to stave off its effects for as long as possible and keep the upper (albeit shaky) hand.

Damn you Parkinson's Disease! However, I was well aware that I was on a different road in life now, and I had no idea where it was taking me.

I started reading up about Parkinson's Disease on the internet and the overriding message was that everyone's symptoms and speed of progression are different, so I stopped. This was MY journey and I was going to deal with it one day at a time in my own way. Keeping active seemed the most important thing to do at this stage, so I decided to make that my priority.

I called my trusty MSK physio to tell him my news and to congratulate him on his prophecy all those months ago when he repeated over and over that something wasn't right - he was completely, totally, utterly right. He promised to be right there for me to keep my wobbly limbs moving.

Boy, had he drawn the short straw I thought! He was going to have his work cut out for him - especially as I had a bad dose of frozen shoulder emerging on my Parkinson's side.

When I saw my neuro physio a few days later he had passed on the diagnosis. She was a little surprised as she reckoned I presented slightly differently from a standard 'parky' and I had to agree. When I'd done my little bits of online reading to try to figure out what was wrong I didn't seem to quite fit the bill, but I do tend to avoid following the crowd in life so nothing new there! However, it was early days, so perhaps my PD would get more typical as it developed.

Mrs. Neuro Physio invited me to join a weekly physiotherapist led neuro pilates class that she was running with a colleague. I had tried a yoga class at our local community centre when I'd first got the tremor and was feeling increasingly stiff. I thought it might help, but I was so self-conscious every time I got the wobbles that I gave up. Neuro pilates sounded perfect though, so I jumped at the chance.

It was difficult deciding whether to or how to tell people about my diagnosis, and everyone is different in this respect. I admire those that soldier on without saying a word until they really have to because it's become too hard to hide their symptoms. I tend to be the opposite and like to be open about everything, but I also didn't want to make a big thing of it. I opted to just tell my closest friends at first, let the word spread a bit, then tell other people as and when the opportunity arose.

The most difficult was how to handle it with my by then, 16 year-old son. He was at the most important stage of his school career, about to sit his Higher exams. A year previously he had already had to deal with the diagnosis of my genetic heart defect and go through the ordeal of being tested himself to see if he had inherited it (he hadn't thank God), so this was the last thing he needed and I didn't want to rock his boat any more. On the other hand, I didn't want to hide it from him, especially as other people knew. I chose my moment carefully and raised the issue stressing I was absolutely fine just now, which I was, and would be for a long time to come. I figured if I didn't seem particularly bothered, he wouldn't be either. He took it all in his stride as he always does. He's a bright kid and I knew he would Google it if he wanted to.

As word spread about my Parkinson's it was interesting to witness the different reactions from people - friends, family, colleagues, and health professionals. One nurse practitioner's reaction was priceless. I had gone to see her about getting a steroid injection to help my frozen shoulder – the third bout I'd had of that incredibly painful condition. She was very efficient and business-like in her approach and then asked me to stand up so she could manipulate it. 'Which arm?' she said.

'My parky arm.' I replied.

'I'm sorry?' she retorted looking at me quizzically having clearly not read my notes.

'I have Parkinson's Disease' I said, 'The frozen shoulder is on my Parkinson's affected side.'

All of a sudden her whole demeanour changed and gushingly overcompensating she launched into 'Oh my goodness, how awful for you,

you poor thing, that's dreadful, that's the last thing you need with Parkinson's, we'll need to get you sorted, dear oh dear, how unfair...'.

It was both hilarious and somehow a little disappointing at the same time.

I respect the fact that some people are open, interested, and sympathetic, some don't know what to say and others simply don't want to say anything. I tried and still do, to go along with whatever 'vibe' I am getting from a person. If they seem interested and ask questions I will openly answer them, if not I'll keep quiet. I don't think any more or less of those that do or those that don't want to talk about it, it's a very personal thing. The last thing I want to do is make anyone feel uncomfortable.

8. FINDING MY WAY

About three weeks after diagnosis day I got a call from the Parkinson's nurse arranging to come and visit me at home. What a marvellous service I thought! I felt quite spoiled not having to trek to the hospital and was looking forward to talking to her since I had now had time to get my head together. I had plenty of questions I wanted to ask.

It quickly transpired that she lived in the same village as we had previously, so had quite a number of mutual acquaintances. It was nice to hear about them and some of the changes in the village since we had moved away, and she told me she was due to retire in two months and was moving away soon too. I heard how she was going to stay near her daughter and would be looking after her grandchildren because her daughter had got a new job. Half an hour had passed and I knew all about each grandchild, their ages, names, shoe size and little foibles, the ins and outs of her house sale, why she chose the house she was to be moving to, how she was going to decorate it, and what felt like her daughter's entire new job description.

I was starting to get quite twitchy, glancing repeatedly at the clock. She still hadn't mentioned Parkinson's - time was rapidly ticking by and there was so much I wanted to ask and say. Suddenly, I had a moment of genius and in a rare gap in her monologue I chipped in, 'So when you leave do you know who my Parkinson's nurse will be?' At last I'd managed to steer the conversation towards the matter in hand, not that it was overly successful since she said no, but at least we were finally on the right road!

I asked about treatments and she told me in very broad terms about the main line of medication - levodopa - which was developed in the 1960s and still remains the first point of call. She was quite vague and downbeat about the options available, which was worrying, and complained that her job was made much more difficult because of the lack of new treatments. She said that often there wasn't a lot she could really do other than help people find the right balance of drugs and offer moral support. She really wasn't selling the Parkinson's Nurse service to me!

I then got a random story based on what seemed to be purely anecdotal evidence, that there was a cluster of cases in our area and strangely it appeared to target middle class, active, creative people.

She gave me the website address for the charity Parkinson's UK and said anything I wanted to know I'd find out there. With that she gathered her stuff, bid her farewell, and left saying she would send me some leaflets.

© Parkinson's UK
Reproduced with kind permission of Parkinson's UK, a registered charity in England and Wales (258197) and Scotland (SC037554).

Well, that was a pretty useless hour of my life I wouldn't get back. I was annoyed and disappointed. I am very wary about what I read on the Internet, especially when it comes to health issues but it looked like the Parkinson's UK website was going to have to be my 'nurse' so I turned to it. The one message that seemed to shine through was what I'd originally thought - try to keep active. I have always enjoyed squash, swimming, running, and biking so I thought 'I can do that!'.

© Parkinson's UK
Reproduced with kind permission of Parkinson's UK, a registered charity in England and Wales (258197) and Scotland (SC037554).

Ha! Not so! Catch number 1. Parkinson's brings with it bouts of utter fatigue when lifting your toothbrush is an effort let alone jogging round the block. Catch number 2. Your affected limbs have a mind of their own on occasions which can have interesting consequences.

I had now put on heaps of weight since breaking my ankle and the subsequent health palaver involving my heart, then this infernal disease - so I felt to try to shed some pounds, and for my general well-being, I needed to do some cardio. I took to the treadmill. I'd been running the best part of three-quarters of a marathon a couple of years previously - I knew my new 'bionic' metal ankle couldn't take that kind of distance anymore so I set myself a conservative target of 10k.

Try as I might though, it just wasn't happening. I initially blamed it on being out of condition and the fact that I was carrying around the equivalent of a small heifer that I hadn't had before, but it wasn't that. It was that rhythm thing - even on a treadmill my right leg would randomly stall or stutter. When that almost caused me to propel off the back of the treadmill, I decided I needed to adopt another approach.

Ah! Swimming - perfect! No - triple fail:

1. My costume was now so tight it was crying for mercy at the seams before I even reached the water.

2. Does a one-legged duck swim in circles? One weak side versus a straight lane. I say no more!

3. I thought I was going to have to call the fire brigade to get me back out of my overstretched costume when I got out of the pool!

I decided to see how my new neuro pilates class went and take things from there. There were eight of us in the class with a range of neurological issues from Stroke to Multiple Sclerosis and one other person, perhaps about 10 or so years older than me, with Parkinson's. I was probably the youngest at 52, ranging up to a wonderful lady heading for her mid-eighties. My fabulous neuro physio and her equally fabulous colleague led the class with one at the front showing us what to do, and the other keeping an eye on us, helping when required, and offering alternative exercises if anyone was struggling. I came away from the first session absolutely shocked to the core by how much range, flexibility, strength, and control I had already lost in my Parkinson's (right) side.

Pictures with the kind permission of H & W Physiotherapy and my lovely classmates!

I realised that neuro pilates was not going to be just beneficial it was going to be vital. I was hooked. They also happened to be the nicest bunch of people I had met in a very long time!

Needless to say, with every good comes a bad - an envelope of leaflets arrived from the Parkinson's nurse mostly about things like how to cope with a feeding tube, mobility devices, and support for carers. What?! Make me feel rubbish why don't you! I really didn't need to read that at this stage in the game. I was furious and threw them in the bin!

9. REALITY CHECK

At the end of July 2017, I had my three months post-diagnosis appointment with the GP. It was the usual lovely lady whom I'd been seeing for many years and knew me well. I could tell she was genuinely hurting for me that I'd had such a horrendous run of serious health issues and that getting PD at the age of 52 was just downright unlucky.

By that age, 'young' is not a word you really associate with yourself, but I officially have 'Young Onset Parkinson's', the label given to those of working age with the disease. I quite liked the sound of that because I'm certain the mention of Parkinson's Disease conjures up for most people the image of a little old shrivelled tremoring person in a bath-chair with a tartan rug over their knees.

Of course, most people want some kind of prognosis for their illness but the GP reiterated what I'd read on the Parkinson's UK website - that everyone is affected differently both in their variety of symptoms and the speed at which the symptoms develop. However, she had a caveat.

'You're a strong, positive thinking, intelligent woman - I personally firmly believe that will count for an awful lot in the months and years to come. Stay positive and don't give in.' she said.

I was very flattered by her description - I just think of me as, well, just being me, kind of normal run of the mill really - so it gave me a little unexpected boost!

She already knew about my ongoing physiotherapy and I told her about my new neuro pilates class. 'I rest my case.' she smiled.

I explained that I still didn't feel I was doing enough to help myself and asked for occupational therapy to assist with some of the problems I was having at work, like typing and writing, but apparently that's a bit beyond their remit - getting dressed and making a cup of tea are the kind of things they supposedly focus on. Okay, we'll save that for later! However, she offered to refer me to an NHS neuro physiotherapist at the local hospital to see if she could add anything to what I was already doing physiotherapy-wise.

It turned out the NHS physio was running a fortnightly exercise session for anyone with neurological issues, which took the form of a mini-circuits exercise class. Two minutes at ten different 'stations' doing things like step-ups, hand weights, twists, heel raises, etc. I thought this more cardio-related session would complement well the core strength and flexibility focus of the private neuro pilates class I was going to.

There were just two or three participants in the room each week, varying from an elderly Stroke victim to a man in his forties in a wheelchair with no lower limbs. I was streets ahead of the others physically and at times I found it awkward and quite honestly rather inappropriate to be in the same session. I had to work hard at focusing on why I was there and what I was doing to divert my mind from the guilt I was feeling about my ability or lack of *disability* compared to theirs. Sometimes I would purposefully make 'ooh, this is difficult' noises and huff and puff, just to try to make them feel better. I could see the benefit of what I was doing though and put my heart and soul into it. The physio found my determination amusing and had to regularly tell me not to overdo it, especially after I did nearly two hundred heal raises at break-neck speed, then got such incredibly sore calves I couldn't walk properly for about three days! We were developing a good relationship and always enjoyed a chat and a laugh at the end of each class.

A big eye-opener came for me about week three when a very apprehensive, self-conscious looking young man with a straggly beard arrived accompanied by what looked like his Granny. He had to be coaxed in and I smiled at him gently trying to be encouraging. He was quite disabled, particularly on one side, and seemed to have little control over his shaking somewhat contorted limbs. I thought perhaps he had Cerebral Palsy. The physio gave him a lot of support that session and I could tell he was a troubled soul. My heart really went out to him. His Granny came to collect him at the end, and I wondered if he would actually come back.

A fortnight later I was waiting in the corridor for the class to start and he reappeared with his Granny again and sat next to me. I was genuinely chuffed to see him.

'Hi, boy am I glad to see you - I was worried I was going to be on my own this week and the physio would work me to the bone!' I said.

That seemed to make him relax a little and we passed the time of day about the weather etc., until we were called in. He was far more at ease this time and we exchanged the odd comment and laugh as the session went on. I was really pleased he felt comfortable with me.

The next time he arrived, he immediately smiled when he spotted me which was nice. I was ready to make pleasant small talk when instead he suddenly came out with, 'You've got Parkinson's Disease haven't you?'

I replied 'Yes, I have - well spotted.', ready to launch into my tale of woe about Young Onset, diagnosed at 52, bla, bla - but he took the wind right out of my sail before I could say another word.

'Not difficult to spot' he said sadly, 'So have I. I'm 23 - I've had Parkinson's since I was 19.'

I was totally, utterly gob-smacked, and I desperately hoped my face hadn't displayed the shock I felt.

'Oh my God' I said, 'That's so unfair!' He nodded disconsolately. I could feel tears pricking my eyes.

He played on my mind a lot in between sessions and over the coming weeks I learned from him first-hand the horrifying reality of this bastard (excuse my language) disease. He spoke of the horrendous side effects of the drugs, his daily battle to simply get washed and dressed, the frightening hallucinations that had started to plague him, and the trouble he was having swallowing his food.

He was tortured watching his peers going forth in life and building futures for themselves whilst his life was spiralling into decline. He had already had his driving licence withdrawn for medical reasons less than four years after having passed his test and was in and out of hospital. He was understandably a very sad person and made no bones about it - it was complete and utter shit. I felt so desperately sorry for him and insanely angry that life could be so cruel.

10. SADDLE SORES

Sadly, as all good things do, my physio sessions courtesy of the NHS were to come to an end. For some inexplicable reason, you are allowed eight and that's your lot. Well, actually not inexplicable at all, in that it is obviously an issue of resources. But surely in the long run it would be a saving to provide Parkinson's patients with the one intrinsic thing linked to a good prognosis - exercise.

Parkinson's Disease conspires to do everything it possibly can to slow you down and limit your movement. Exercise not only fends off all manner of ills that lack of it brings the general population - weight gain, cardiovascular issues, diabetes, etc., but with PD it can help avoid falls from compromised balance, maintain general mobility leading to less reliance on drugs, a better quality of life and longer independence, assist the typically sluggish digestive system of a parky to keep moving (!), support mental health... The list goes on and on.

As it turned out, my last session happened to also be the physio's last session as she was retiring. I was sad to be saying goodbye especially as she'd done one really special thing for me.

Not long after we met, I was having a good wholesome moan to her about my running and swimming failures and how much I missed being active. I told her I had even bitten the bullet and got back on my bike despite having wrecked my ankle on my last foray into two wheels. But being a wimp wasn't going to get me anywhere, so I'd made myself do it. I was pretty terrified, but it didn't take long before that feeling of fresh air and freedom that I'd missed so much came flooding back. It was far from plain sailing. Firstly, I was carrying a new set of bingo wings, a few spare tyres, and a pair of thighs that would kick start a jumbo jet, since the last time I was on a saddle, so it was hard going. Secondly, since we live in Scotland rather than Holland, everywhere you look there's a hill staring back at you. And lastly, my body seemed to have started this silly lark of plunging to 'energy zero' in a matter of seconds, generally at the furthest point from home. It really got me down. I mean really. I was extremely worried I'd end up stranded somewhere.

Beautiful hilly Scotland. Photo © Murray Macfarlane

She listened patiently then said, 'What about getting an electric bike, it'll give you some back-up when you need it.'

Well, I have to say that was the best idea anyone has ever had in the history of good ideas!

As it happened, one of my best friends, who clearly was a total genius without me realising it, already had an e-bike so I called her up and asked for a try. One short trip and I was hooked!

I immediately got myself a shiny new e-bike, as I said before - you can't put a price on your health - and it was the new love of my life! It was my oasis, it gave me back my freedom and with it a new lease of life. My friend and I started covering many miles together around the gorgeous local country roads - her with her arthritic knee and me with my parky wobbles! What a pair! (Just for the record, the battery doesn't do all the work for you - it just lends a kindly helping hand when you need it - bless it!)

I cycled to my next session with the physio after I got it and went in with my cycle gear and helmet on. She took one look at me and went rushing out into the car park to look at it and hugged me! We shed a tear together as I thanked her from the bottom of my heart for her idea.

My bike is more than three years old now and I love it as much as the day I got it. I always hope I will bump into her some time so she can see I'm still enjoying it.

Every day I was learning just a little bit more about how to live with Parkinson's, but I was also coming to realise there are more ups and downs than the world's best rollercoaster. There are good days and not so good days - I try not at this point to call them bad days - I'm keeping the 'b' word for later or I may run out of negative vocabulary as this infernal disease progresses! And that's another thing - I also refuse to call it an illness, I prefer to use the word 'condition'. I don't see myself as ill more just malfunctioning.

The variations don't just come about by days though, they come by hours - I get up feeling fine, then suddenly realise I'm not anymore. Either my tremor has gone wild or every scrap of energy has left me. Try as I might to fight it, I am slowly getting better at accepting it. When the plug gets pulled on my energy it is invariably accompanied by a rip-roaring headache. I often wonder if it's the result of the tension in my muscles from trying to control the tremor until I can get a rest.

A lot of people, including some health professionals, don't realise that Parkinson's, even in a mild form like mine at present can be painful. I was working at home one day glued to my computer doing accounts. My tremor was pretty bad, so I was struggling to type and move papers around. Increasingly, I kept having to stop, stretch, and walk around but as is my way, I got engrossed in it and didn't take enough stretch breaks. The most awful muscle spasm set in down my arm and leg, it was so sore! Lesson learned the hard way. I mentioned it to the doctor and he gave me some Diazepam to have in reserve for any future bad muscle spasms. It works reasonably well and takes the worst away - but it's not conducive to getting my accounts finished as it makes me both tired and pleasantly chilled! I try not to take it unless I really have to.

11. BLOGGING IT

As Parkinson's became increasingly lodged in my everyday existence, I felt I wanted to share my experiences with anyone interested in finding out what it was all about for an everyday person in an everyday life. I had joined a few Parkinson's forums on Facebook and noticed how much the Parkinson's community rely on each other for information, help, and support. I felt this was, without a doubt, indicative of the fact that it feels so much like 'the forgotten disease.' There is absolutely nothing 'sexy' about Parkinson's for the media nor sadly, it seems, drug companies either. You hear so much about Cancer and Cardiology but so little about neurological issues - perhaps Multiple Sclerosis somewhat more than PD. Is it because it is generally regarded as an old person's disease?

From an entirely personal perspective, I'd had plenty of dealings with the cardiology department of our main large hospital through my own inherited heart issues and those of my father before me. Somehow it appeared to be a different world altogether. The cardiology department was brand spanking new, teeming with people, and seemed to change every five minutes with the addition of a new wing, or new equipment. Neurology felt dowdy and lifeless in comparison, even the staff seemed more dour! Now, this might be entirely my imagination, or simply a feature of our local services, but it felt very real.

Having spent fifteen years as a broadcast journalist and having an academic author for a father, writing is part of my make up, so I decided to write a Facebook blog. Additionally, and entirely selfishly it would be an outlet for me! 'Just Wobbling Along' was born in October 2017.

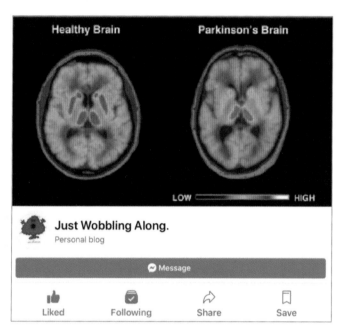

I thought if nobody reads it that's fine, but if it helps one person then it's been worthwhile. I suppose as well, it was a good way to keep friends and extended family I don't see often, in touch with what was happening to me. I knew nothing about Parkinson's Disease before it enveloped me in its evil clutches and it was extremely evident that I wasn't alone, so general education was a big incentive too - getting the word out there. I had a bit of backtracking to do to bring the blog up to date with where my PD stood at that point, then I simply started sharing my journey on it every now and then.

Like this book, it wasn't about the latest research or medical treatments, that I leave entirely to the experts, but it was about the personal challenges, emotions, and dilemmas. The first post on 17th October 2017 attracted almost fifty views - admittedly I'd invited a lot of my Facebook friends to read it, but all the same, I was extremely chuffed! After a while I started sharing it with one or two Parkinson's forums on Facebook and the readership started to grow. People in the same rocky PD boat started to respond which was becoming both interesting and informative. Apart from the two sufferers I'd met at my physio classes this was my only contact with other Parkinson's people, and I was learning more from them than any doctor, nurse, or Google search.

Inevitably it also made me starkly aware that I was still really only dipping my toe into the Parkinson's pond and realistically what lay ahead of me was a downward spiral that would most likely end up ravaging my body and mind. It is the latter I fear by far the most.

The courage of so many of the people who communicated with my page was astounding, and I can only hope I have half their fight and spirit in years to come.

Just Wobbling Along readers were popping up in all corners of the world and comparing medical services fascinated me. Needless to say, although so far my neurological experience of our precious NHS compared poorly to my cardiology one, I still felt very lucky that money will never be an obstacle in getting the treatment I need - although I say that in slight trepidation of what future Governments might do.

As I write this, Just Wobbling Along is attracting an audience of more than five thousand – beyond my wildest expectations!

I have never paid to boost its coverage, even though Facebook keep trying to get money out of me – they clearly don't realise they are dealing with a true born and bred canny Scot! I can only hope therefore, I must be doing something right to be blessed with so much coverage.

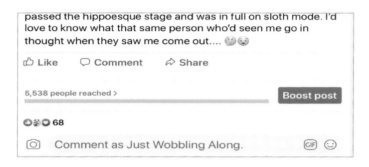

More than anything though, I'd especially like the blog and this book, to reach more health professionals of all disciplines. I respect each and every one of them for their knowledge and expertise but so far very few seem to have a real handle on Parkinson's – the specialists apart of course. I absolutely don't intend that to sound insulting, and totally understand that they can't know everything about every disease, but Parkinson's is a real oddball to understand!

The effects are so varied, apart from the motor problems there is the array of non-motor problems (more about that later), then there are the drugs which are a whole minefield of their own. Perhaps unlike very many other diseases, Parkinson's 'the medical textbook' version does not even scratch the surface of Parkinson's 'the reality'. If I had £5 for every time I've wanted to say 'Yes, in theory, but it doesn't actually work like that in real life.' I'd be very rich. I am sure many of my fellow parkies will identify with that.

Through the blog, I have 'met' some amazing, well informed, articulate, stoic, and dedicated sufferers and carers. Social media may have many failings, indeed I am not its greatest fan in many respects but for this purpose, it is absolutely fantastic. What on earth did ill people do before the Internet?

Of course, like anything you read in newspapers and magazines, or see on television, always exercise a degree of caution and judgement, and have a bit of a thick skin - but on the whole, there is far more to be gained from online support groups than to be lost.

Never forget though - there is always an 'off' button! Overexposure to your medical demons can be as dangerous as no outlet for them at all.

12. OBSTACLES ABOUND

Saturday 4th November 2017

It may be hard to imagine, but there are funny sides to Parkinson's - well at least there still are for me, although I'm sure those further down this rocky road will not agree. My time will come.

However, I was amused to discover that I couldn't wave anymore. I put up my hand to do it one day, but the side-to-side thing just didn't happen, and instead turned into a kind of nerdy salute! Any form of repetitive movement tends to stall with a parky. In future, I need to remember to use my left hand, or perhaps I'll practice a slow regal lift of my right arm with a gentle move of the palm like the Queen!

Another new little foible I've developed is an issue going through a heavy door like that in a shop. I haul it open as you do, and march through entirely unaware that my door opening right arm hasn't come through with me! It's only when my arm is about to snap that I screech (vocally as well) to a halt and everyone behind me piles into each other like dominoes. It is very embarrassing, and I generally get a lot of huffs and puffs from the people behind. I ought to think about wearing some sort of hazard sign. Instead of those stickers you get on disabled cars that say, 'Hand Controls in Operation' I should have a hi-vis vest that says, 'No Limb Control in Operation.'!

Simple things are no longer simple anymore. Off I went to the hairdresser thinking to myself, 'What could possibly go wrong?'. First of all, as every parky knows, the thing that makes your tremor worst is trying not to tremor. This leads to a vicious circle of tensing up, getting pain, trying to relax, and general fidgeting about trying to get comfortable, pain-free, and not attract attention. Sitting still is so incredibly difficult. I'm sure people must think I desperately need the toilet or must suffer from ADHD!

Coffee, some magazines, and relax... Not a chance! I can't use both hands to hold the magazine or I'll get seasick trying to read it as it wobbles before my eyes. It'll also turn heads as the fluttering of the pages gives everyone around me a free blow-dry. The solution: balance it on my knee and hold/turn the pages with my good hand. The result: the magazine falls on the floor when I reach for my coffee! Next time I think I'll just stick with the coffee and forget the magazine. I never have a clue who all the so-called celebrities in the magazines are anyway.

I should also mention - *mental note - when sitting, only ever cross your legs with the wobbly foot firmly planted on the ground. The consequence of letting it swing free I discovered was not good at all when my parky limb did one of its uncontrollable jerks and kicked the poor hairdresser in the shins. Oh blimey...

The other thing I unwittingly went to without putting in any prior Parkinson's thought was a Service of Remembrance followed by an awards ceremony and reception.

It all started to go downhill the moment I arrived and immediately realised that sitting sandwiched between strangers in a row is like a red rag to a bull for a tremor - it just had to go wild because it knew I really didn't want it to. I swear it has a truly evil mind of its own! I tried sitting on my hand, clasping my hands, folding my arms, gripping my hand, not gripping my hand, relaxing my arm, tensing my arm. Nope, it was just not going to stop! On the contrary, it was bringing the entire right side of my body along with it. I wasn't remotely paying attention to the service, all I could think about was combatting the wobbles. Do I offer the people around me an embarrassed explanation? Do I give them an apologetic look? Or do I adopt an air of 'tremor, what tremor...?', and try not to grimace too much at the cramping pain starting to sear up my arm and down my leg.

Then came the realisation that holding the Order of Service sheet was a no go unless everyone around me was happy to have their hair re-arranged by what morphed into a fan. The words for the hymns were on the sheet so I went for damage limitation and held it in my left hand, which although not tremoring itself, still caused a slight fanning of the surrounds because of the shake down my whole right side.

'Please stand for a minute's silence.' said the Minister.

Everybody respectfully rose to their feet and stood stock still like statues, except the jiggering idiot in the middle of the congregation that was ME - getting steadily more light-headed from the effort of trying not to be a jiggering idiot. Thank goodness most of the people had their eyes shut at that point.

Then came the reception and I optimistically thought the torture would be over. Wrong! As soon as I entered immediate panic set in as everyone was filing in shaking the hands of the various dignitaries. Oh no! a) my hand was quivering and sweaty from the ordeal of the service and b) it doesn't do up and down movements anymore. Dilemma! Should I offer my left hand? No, that'll look really stupid. Should I offer none at all? No, that'll appear ridiculous and rude. I had no choice - I pathetically offered my rigid clammy right hand and left them to do the up and down thing while holding what must have felt like a sticky dead fish with rigor mortis.

Next was the buffet 'challenge' - easy decision - politely decline any refreshments or I and everyone around me will be wearing them within seconds of me shakily taking hold of a glass or plate. Shame, I do hate missing out on food.

I was utterly knackered by the time the ordeal was over.

I really need to start thinking ahead so that I'm more prepared for the challenges different occasions will present for me now, ones I previously wouldn't have given a second thought. But hey, it's not the end of the world, I can do that.

Oh, I ought to mention the other thing that is now a real no go - any self-service coffee or food outlet that requires you to carry a tray. Give me a tray and I swear I can get its contents to land on the floor quicker than you can say, 'two cappuccinos please'. I suppose I could go into an embarrassing explanation of having Parkinson's and ask if someone could carry it to my table for me, but without putting too fine a point on it I'd feel an utter twat. I'm also sure that unless I was wearing a sandwich board saying, 'I have Parkinson's Disease' people would be giving me the evil 'Spock eye' thinking, 'What's so special about her', or worse, they'd be transmitting a death wish from further back in the queue if the only member of staff left their station behind the self-service counter to deliver my tray for me. Life is too short to deal with that and I guess it saves me lots of money on over-priced beverages.

13. TRYING TO REASON

As 2018 dawned I found that in my quiet moments I would wonder, how did this happen? Not in an anguished or angry way, just a curious way. Since there seems to be little clue as to why people get Parkinson's, it intrigues me. I have quite excelled myself getting it though, as it is apparently very much more a man's disease – indeed it is thought around fifty percent more males than females have it.

There are various proven gene mutations associated with Parkinson's, so a minority of people are known to have inherited it. Although I have been tested and found to have a faulty MYBPC 3 gene, which has caused my inherited heart condition Hypertrophic Cardiomyopathy, I have never been tested for any of the known Parkinson's related gene defects. My official diagnosis is Idiopathic Parkinson's meaning no known cause. Perhaps I should get tested - I have thought about it even though I don't know of anyone in my family who had Parkinson's.

There are many theories as to what may cause the disease in non-inherited cases. Some say it's possibly a digestive thing to do with your body not absorbing what's needed to produce dopamine in your brain, others that there could be an environmental factor such as chemicals or pesticides that we inhale or absorb.

That then makes me reflect on all the substances with which we knowingly and more worryingly, unknowingly, pollute our bodies, that could have caused it. Have I had a reaction to the processed foods I've eaten, the synthetic fibres I've worn, the make-up I've put on, deodorants, shampoos, car fumes - the list is endless? Or was it something that happened in the womb? The full dangers of smoking in pregnancy weren't appreciated when I was born in the mid-sixties and my mother smoked throughout. She was also taken quite ill shortly after I was born so I was not breastfed, but fed on formula milk - maybe it was that?

I wonder therefore if the incidence of Parkinson's is lower amongst remote tribal folk in Africa or Eskimos, living simply on what nature provides? Well, it's too late for me to consider becoming a self-sufficient organic eating recluse on an uninhabited Scottish island. Was I a few decades younger and knew anything about science, I'd perhaps go and investigate, but I'm not and I don't, so I'll just have to wonder some more!

Purely in my own case, I can't help wondering whether my heart defect and my Parkinson's are linked. There is absolutely no substance to this theory other than my own gut feeling, and the fact that they both became symptomatic for me at the same time. A protein called Alpha Synuclein seems to pop up in articles I've read on both diseases but since I have no scientific training or knowledge whatsoever, this may be entirely arbitrary.

Although the question of cause is always at the back of my mind I do get irritated with what seem to be constant headlines from around the world of one breakthrough or another, that are always followed by a 'but' - 'but' these are results in mice, 'but' these are early indications, 'but' clinical trials have not yet started. I am deeply thankful to every single scientist working on this, and there are not nearly enough of them compared to many other diseases, but it is soul-destroying having hopes raised and quashed by exaggerated media headlines.

I look forward to the day when a very clever person comes up with the real answer, and I am 100% certain they will. I desperately hope that's sooner rather than later though, as it may also be the key to unlocking a cure and preventing other people from suffering this hellish affliction. I am confident the breakthrough will come in my lifetime although I believe I will be too far down the road to benefit. Nevertheless, it will make me the happiest person in the world when it does.

If I could wave a magic wand would I have my PD taken away? Well, of course, I don't want this cursed affliction, but if there is some kind of quota of diseases that has to be shared between everyone then I reckon I'm a good candidate. I am lucky enough to have the wherewithal to deal with it (I think - hope?!), I have great family and friends around me, and I don't have to worry about how I'm going to afford to feed and clothe myself.

So, on that basis, why not me - I accept the challenge I've been given and hope it spares someone less fortunate from getting it.

14. TWO LEFT HANDS

A year since diagnosis and every day was becoming a learning experience. This Parkinson's journey I'd embarked upon was certainly not turning out to be a long straight road of slow decline but more a twisting turning rollercoaster of ups and downs. Good days and less good days for no explicable reason.

As yet I was unmedicated - a parky in its raw natural state!

There are two schools of thought on medicating Parkinson's, going on anecdotal evidence from the many people from around the world who have commented on my blog posts.

Some seem to think that holding off as long as possible is best as the drugs lose their efficacy the longer you are on them, not to mention the many side effects associated with them - more on that later. Others are of the opinion that taking them early after diagnosis may help slow down the progression of the disease. I get the feeling the latter is a rather older school of thought. It also seems to vary depending on where you live. My American blog friends seem to be more medicated than my UK ones, but that's just a personal observation.

My own feeling was that I didn't want to take any medication unless I felt I had reached a stage where I really had to. This doesn't only relate to PD drugs, I feel similarly about all medication. It is, at the end of the day, another chemical going into your body. Anyway, it was probably just as well I wasn't wanting to pop any pills since I hadn't heard a tweet from the neurologist or Parkinson's nurse!

Although my PD was posing many little issues, they were more annoyances rather than real problems, and one way or another they were all surmountable with a bit of thought. So, although I'm sure I will have, at this stage in the game I didn't feel I had too much to moan about. It was also quite comforting to know that there was medication waiting in the wings for when I might need it.

One of the things about Parkinson's is that it's right there in your consciousness every waking minute of every day. Some illnesses like for example my heart condition, as long as they're not giving you grief at a particular moment you can forget they're there. Not so, I feel with Parkinson's, because it affects your movement, especially when you are still unmedicated.

A lot of the time I found myself doing a kind of juggling act between my right and left hands. It is quite amazing how the body starts to adjust to having a defective right side. I was now naturally picking up a pen with my left hand and was washing my car one day and suddenly realised I was doing it with my left hand. I have no recollection of swapping from my right hand, it had just happened!

Some things don't come quite so easily though. Spreading butter or jam is one of them. For some reason, my left hand doesn't seem willing to learn this particular task and I end up performing a variety of plate swappings and knife

swappings, that make a lot of mess and end up with my pet hate - the corners of the bread not covered!

 However, on a good day, my right hand was still managing to do it and the wobbly result was actually rather decorative. It almost looks like I meant it!

Things like this, that are obviously the product of much wobbliness, have become known in our house as 'crinkle-cut'! If there's sugar spilled on the counter my husband will say mockingly, rolling his eyes, 'Ah, crinkle-cut sugar.'

Often, I'll use a phrase like, 'I'll do it later, I'm too crinkle-cut just now.' – meaning my tremor is too bad at that point. Being able to laugh at yourself is so important in surviving this parky game.

Another important job my left-hand won't play ball with and do, is brush my teeth. The first challenge, if I'm really shaky, is getting the toothpaste onto the brush rather than every surface around it! I do have an electric toothbrush which is an absolute godsend for any parky, but doing it with my left hand feels all wrong - it's like putting your coat on the opposite arm from normal or going upstairs starting on the opposite foot from usual. I start brushing with my right hand but for some reason, the toothbrush seems to slide out of my hand or I drop it. What I end up with is a kind of two-handed sawing motion with foam pouring from my mouth. Thankfully, I haven't knocked out any teeth - yet.

The normal procedure of washing dishes no longer works either as my right arm doesn't do the scrubbing motion that's needed. I end up holding the sponge still and waggling the plate around on it with my left hand! I'm sure God invented dishwashers for Parkinson's people, so we bought one. Problem solved!

Drying my hair remains a daily challenge! Previously I'd hold the hairdryer with my left hand and style my hair with a brush in my right hand. I've had to give up with the hairdryer altogether after burning my head with it, tangling the brush in my hair, and scorching my opposite hand. I now use a girly hot brush thing which blows and styles in one using a combination of both hands, ending in a result that isn't too scary.

These are all the things I can do myself that nobody sees so they're okay - the ones I detest this infernal condition for are the ones that people can see. Eating is by far the worst. If my tremor is bad it is extremely difficult to use a knife. It taps on the plate and if I'm not careful, does the last thing I want, which is draw attention to myself. I can't do a cutting motion so end up trying to tear food apart. My soup spoon can only be half full and as for peas - it's a miracle if they reach my mouth! Horrid things. They should be banned on the basis that they are too embarrassing for parkies!

People I know well are happy to cut my food for me and I'm slowly getting used to asking - some pals are so good they just do it now as a matter of course without any fuss, bless them! Can you imagine what it feels like though, having to ask for help to eat your food at the age of 52? It's certainly put me off eating out.

Buffets are a complete non-starter as I can't hold a plate and serve myself with the other hand. If it's a sit-down meal I go out of my way to choose dishes I can eat with one hand like curry or something that is in small pieces like scampi - I'd choose that over a piece of fish which needs cutting, or I'd go for a beef stew rather than roast beef or steak. It's an absolute minefield and I end up not enjoying my meal sometimes, because it's either too difficult to eat, I can't have what I really fancy or it's simply too much effort to think it through! All a bit of a disaster for a foodie like me!

A helpful little thing I have, that I also carry about in my handbag in case we ever stop off for an unexpected bite to eat, is my Nelson Knife – a knife and fork in one. It's good for cutting and picking up your food with one hand if you're ever having to sit on your parky hand because it's misbehaving!

I hope I never get stopped by the Police though, they might regard it as an offensive weapon! I must also remember to take it out of my handbag if I'm ever flying anywhere. Try explaining that to airport security.

Every cloud can have a silver lining too though. Parkinson's does at least have one perk.

It was one of my stiffer days and I was slowly pottering around the house catching up on some housework, and decided to tackle the ironing mountain. Even just taking out the ironing board and getting it all set up was an effort at times, but needs must.

Oh woe! I was 'devastated' (not) – I found that I couldn't do it! My parky arm just wouldn't do that back and fore movement you need. What a pity (not), it was one of my favourite jobs (not), such a shame (not). Dear me, someone else will have to do it now.

I gleefully told my blogging pals!

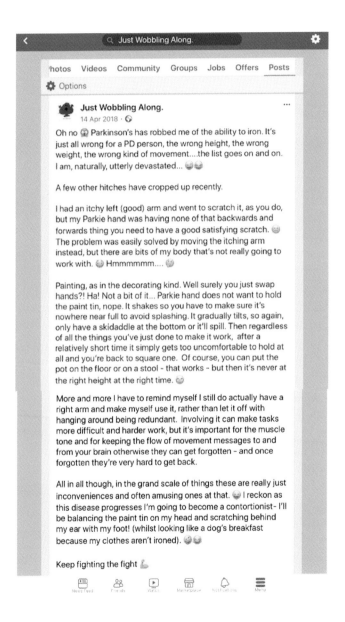

Photos   Videos   Community   Groups   Jobs   Offers   Posts

Options

Just Wobbling Along.
14 Apr 2018 ·

Oh no 😨 Parkinson's has robbed me of the ability to iron. It's just all wrong for a PD person, the wrong height, the wrong weight, the wrong kind of movement....the list goes on and on. I am, naturally, utterly devastated... 😂😂

A few other hitches have cropped up recently.

I had an itchy left (good) arm and went to scratch it, as you do, but my Parkie hand was having none of that backwards and forwards thing you need to have a good satisfying scratch. 😂 The problem was easily solved by moving the itching arm instead, but there are bits of my body that's not really going to work with. 😂 Hmmmmmm.... 😐

Painting, as in the decorating kind. Well surely you just swap hands?! Ha! Not a bit of it... Parkie hand does not want to hold the paint tin, nope. It shakes so you have to make sure it's nowhere near full to avoid splashing. It gradually tilts, so again, only have a skidaddle at the bottom or it'll spill. Then regardless of all the things you've just done to make it work, after a relatively short time it simply gets too uncomfortable to hold at all and you're back to square one. Of course, you can put the pot on the floor or on a stool - that works - but then it's never at the right height at the right time. 😐

More and more I have to remind myself I still do actually have a right arm and make myself use it, rather than let it off with hanging around being redundant. Involving it can make tasks more difficult and harder work, but it's important for the muscle tone and for keeping the flow of movement messages to and from your brain otherwise they can get forgotten - and once forgotten they're very hard to get back.

All in all though, in the grand scale of things these are really just inconveniences and often amusing ones at that. 😐 I reckon as this disease progresses I'm going to become a contortionist- I'll be balancing the paint tin on my head and scratching behind my ear with my foot! (whilst looking like a dog's breakfast because my clothes aren't ironed). 😂😂

Keep fighting the fight 💪

News Feed   Friends   Watch   Marketplace   Notifications   Menu

There are random good 'functional' times too though. I remember one night in particular when I woke up in the early hours and suddenly realised that for longer than I could remember my right arm felt normal - no tremor, no pain, no stiffness - woohoo! For a fleeting moment, I thought perhaps it had all been a terrible mistake or a dream, and that I didn't have Parkinson's at all! That was, of course, entirely ludicrous but it was very nice while it lasted!

Our house is gradually becoming increasingly parky-ised with gadgets that make daily life just a little bit easier:

- Automatic salt and pepper mills – that twisting motion needed for manual ones is really difficult for parky hands.
- Automatic hand soap dispensers – love 'em!
- A sugar dispenser bottle with a spout that tips out an alleged teaspoon worth of sugar – more like half, but I'd drop half from a teaspoon on to the counter anyway, so it saves some mess.
- Keys get left in locks inside the house as putting them in can be quite difficult on a not so good day. Perhaps not the best security but needs must!
- Touch base lamps – much easier than having to fumble around with a switch.
- Tongs for turning and picking up things when I'm cooking. Food falls off wobbly spatulas.
- Lots of extra storage shelves in cupboards so I can grab whatever I need easily rather than having to shift things around to get what I want.
- If it can be washed in a dishwasher or the washing machine it is. Hand washing is kept to a minimum.
- An automatic car!

I am very lucky that stairlifts and bathroom rails are still way down my list, but there are a few things I wish someone would invent:

- An automatic contact lense putter-inner. I have a method of still being able to do this, but I don't think it's going to work forever.
- A washing hanging device – doing it gives me such pain in my parky arm on stiff days
- A hammer you just hold and does the bashing for you. Repeated fast movements aren't in a parky's repertoire.
- A butter spreading device to avoid the embarrassing ripple effect!
- A gift-wrapping machine. Cutting paper straight is not compatible with wobbly parkies, and I even ended up in such a tangle once, the sticky tape got stuck in my hair. Aaaargh!

Onwards and upwards though – it could be a whole lot worse.

15. FROM WITHIN

In life, I have always been of the mind to see problems as challenges and rather than sit back and do nothing, I'll always try to find a solution or at least something that might help. Hence why I was going out of my way to keep up some sort of exercise regime. My efforts to get back into running were still pitiful but between my bike and neuro pilates sessions, I felt I was doing okay on that score.

But what else? I'd started eating a mostly vegetarian diet and also trying to make more effort to listen to my body so I could challenge it when it was good and rest it when it was not so good.

 I still wanted to do more though but seemed to be drawing a blank as to what that might be. I turned to my blog and Parkinson's online forums and picked up a few tips on vitamins and minerals that may help. This is some of my little household collection, a few of which I buy in bulk and decant into jam jars!

Please note – none of this constitutes any form of medical advice, and there is no foundation for the choices other than the fact that they seem to work for me! Vitamin D3 – well, that's good for everyone, but especially so in Scotland where the sun doesn't shine too much. B Vitamins - good for your nervous system. Vitamin K2 - good for heart health as I have a dicky ticker. Vitamin C since it's good for fending off coughs & colds and also, I'm not a great fruit lover - I'd eat a carrot long before an apple any day. Magnesium as apparently, amongst other things, it can help sleep and restless legs, and lastly Zinc for immune support.

My favourite is my morning slurp of a water-based live and active bacteria called Symprove, which I feel has made a big difference. I found out about it from an article on one of the Parkinson's forums. It's sorted the niggling digestive issues I've had for a long time and I also seem to be far better at fending off passing sore throats and snuffles. Again, entirely my personal experience. My husband steals it now though!

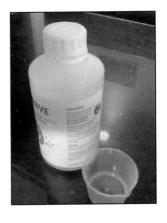

Something that was getting a lot of publicity here in the UK was the decision to legalise CBD products - the oils from Cannabis. I'd heard various stories over the years of people going to America for treatment with Cannabis for various health issues when all else had failed and had recently met a couple locally who swore that it was the only thing that had helped the wife's Multiple Sclerosis. I must stress that the legalised CBD oil in this country has the THC compound removed, which is the psychoactive part that gets you stoned ... more's the pity!

I decided to give it a go. It was a bit of a stab in the dark as suppliers here are not allowed to make any medical claims regarding the product, so there was no information on recommended types or dosages. I went for a middle of the road looking one and placed the order - it wasn't cheap but yet again my mantra 'nothing is more important than your health' came into play. I was quite excited about its arrival even though I was realistic enough to realise it wasn't going to be a magic fix.

It comes in dropper bottles, spray bottles, and capsules but I figured a couple of sprays in my mouth would be easiest. They also offered orange and lemon flavours, but us parkies are hardy souls so I went for the apparently unpleasant-tasting original flavour. I could always have a sweet afterwards to take the taste away... oh well, if I must...! Mind you, I had a worrying afterthought - I hope my breath doesn't smell like I've just had a long drag of a joint.

As it turned out it tasted absolutely foul - like having chewed a cigarette stub that had been lying on the pavement for a week! Definitely orange or lemon flavour next time. A week or so into the experiment I can't say I felt any different, maybe a little bit less tremor and a little more relaxed, but that could be the placebo effect. At least I felt like I was doing something to help myself so would carry on and give it more time. It certainly wasn't doing any harm.

Sadly for me, nothing really noticeable happened over time so I eventually stopped taking it. I can't help wondering if the THC that's removed in this country is the bit that does 'the business'. Perhaps at some point, I'll go somewhere that it is legal to find out. Purely for medicinal purposes, honest. I might have to rename my blog 'Just Floating Along!'.

One tip for a parky using the spray version though – don't attempt to spray it when your tremor is full-on! I successfully missed my mouth one morning and covered the bedroom wall instead. Numerous washings and coats of paint later and its oily presence is still making itself known.

There are, of course, plenty of miracle (usually extortionately priced) substances on the Internet that make bold claims about their powers to combat Parkinson's, but I figure that if they did, the whole Parkinson's community across the world would be jumping for joy. So, in the meantime, I'll refrain from lining some charlatan's pocket and falling for the bogus potions that abound.

I do have some inwardly dreadful cantankerous moments I have to confess... One thing that really winds me up and absolutely shouldn't because it's only people trying to be well-meaning and helpful, is - '...why don't you try this' '...have you tried that' 'I saw this thing on TV that...'. The answer I usually want to scream is, 'Of course I've tried X' or, 'How the heck is X going to help?' Is that the kind of conversation I have to look forward to for the rest of my life? 'My Granny swears by garlic for her arthritis, you should try it.' Aaaargh! I sometimes wish deafness was a symptom of Parkinson's!

While I'm on the subject of the fact that I am a completely horrible person, I may as well mention the most irritating and evil breed of people of all - the normal able-bodied ones who go and do things like running and hillwalking. Bad enough that they have the audacity to do it, but some of them even go as far as telling me about it! My entire being seethes with jealousy and deep hatred oozes out of me. Okay, I exaggerate - but I can't stress enough how difficult it can be sometimes to watch other people doing the things that have been cruelly taken away from me by this Crappinson's Disease, things I would give anything to still be able to do. I totally accept that there are plenty of people who are a million times worse off than me, but especially when I'm having a bad day that doesn't make it any easier.

I can't tell you how bad I feel for admitting that, but it's true and I'm sorry. I expect these kinds of thoughts invade the minds of most people with chronic or incurable conditions or disabilities. They are very isolating and lonely feelings, but they are all part of the journey and I will have to learn to toughen up and deal with them.

I have a lot of friends who take a fit and healthy lifestyle very seriously and I am honestly extremely proud of them. You know who you are, and I am truly sorry for the admission I've made. Don't ever stop what you're doing and don't ever feel guilty for doing it because I've moaned - I really do still love and admire you xx

16. MIXED MUSIC

By now, more than a year after diagnosis my body was adjusting to having to work differently and I was just getting on with things taking each day at a time. I was doing my best to make it no big deal and was pretty switched on to my emotions and the way I felt about this infernal disease - or at least so I thought.

As I've mentioned, music was a big part of my life but PD had already taken away my ability to play the instruments I loved, so when a friend kindly offered to take me to the Parkinson's UK singing therapy group she runs I leapt at the chance. I can still use my voice and I wouldn't need to worry about wobbling while I do it. Perfect - what a great way to get involved in music again - yay!

It was fantastic to see all levels of parkies arriving to take part, from the relatively able-bodied like me, right through to those severely disabled and wheelchair-bound. There must have been forty or more which surprised me - where have all these local Parkinson's people been hiding that I've never met anyone with the disease before? Everyone was welcoming and seemed genuinely interested in me, perhaps particularly so because I seemed to be the youngest person there.

Two lovely ladies took me under their wing and ushered me to a seat in between them. It takes quite a while to organise things when wheelchairs, carers, walking sticks, and generally wobbly people are involved, so we got chatting in the meantime.

'Well, it's marvellous that you've come along and joined us.' said the lady on the right kindly, 'We've got quite a schedule haven't we?' she continued, addressing her friend. 'You get Helga the form for the hydrotherapy and I'll tell her about all the other things she'll be doing.'

It sounded like I had inadvertently joined a club not a choir as she went on. 'On Mondays, we do dancing, gentle exercise class on Tuesday, then on Wednesdays, it's our weekly meeting with a guest speaker once a month. We've had some lovely things like a lady who came and showed us her beautiful basket weaving and an amazing chap who spent a year travelling in his campervan.'

As she completed the rest of the week's activities the other lady re-appeared with the hydrotherapy form.

'Wow.' I said reeling somewhat, 'I had no idea there was so much happening for Parkinson's people.'

'Oh yes, and tea and biscuits after every session.' she added proudly.

Oh my! I felt quite bamboozled as the singing got underway. My music therapist friend did a fantastic job with the class, including speech and vocal exercises which are particularly important for those with more advanced forms of the disease, plus some well-chosen 'sing-along' type songs. Everyone was clearly thoroughly enjoying themselves putting heart and soul into it. It was wonderful to see.

So why then, once I got home, did I sink into one of the biggest downers I've had since starting this PD journey?

I couldn't understand it. I should have been pleased to meet other Parkinson's people and see that I am not alone on this journey - and I was. I should have been pleased to discover there are so many classes and activities for Parkinson's people - and I was. It didn't make any sense, but it really had knocked me sideways.

Then the penny dropped! I want to live LIFE - not live PARKINSON'S. I'm not there yet, nowhere near it, I hope!

I want to swim 50 lengths of the pool not go to hydrotherapy, and I want to cycle 50 miles around the beautiful roads this country has to offer - not sit on a chair doing gentle exercises. I am not willing to hand my life over to this disease for a long time to come if I can help it. I am sure I will have to one day, I suppose it'll be unavoidable due to the inevitable decline that lies ahead - but right now I'm just not in that place. I decided not to go back to the choir and awkwardly explained to my friend what had happened. She totally understood as good friends always do, and I was very grateful to her.

The time had come to decide what to do with all the musical instruments and equipment I had built up over the years, which were standing redundant in my studio in the loft. I'd had it specially built by a very talented musician friend of mine who also happened to be a very talented joiner, so he knew exactly how to make it the perfect music space. It was my oasis. Time seemed to be in a different dimension when I was in there – I'd go up at 7pm and suddenly it was 2am! But it was getting harder and harder to see all my precious instruments and not be able to play them. There was no choice, they were all going to have to go, so I reluctantly decided to sell them.

There were boxes and boxes of music, some of which I'd had since childhood, and instruments galore - keyboards, a trombone, a flute, an oboe, harmonicas, guitars - then all the electrical stuff like mixers, speakers, amps, stage lights. The list was enormous, and it was going to be such a wrench parting with them, worst of all my beloved trumpet and my amazing Nord keyboard.

I'd had my trumpet since 1984 and it was like an extension of me - it was the tool of my trade for a while when I played professionally and we'd been so many places and done so many things together. It had seen action and had years of battle scars, all of which held precious memories.

My Nord keyboard was a far more recent addition, but it was the most amazing thing I've ever owned! It opened up a whole new world of music and sound for me and I had so much still to explore with it that sadly I wouldn't be able to do.

After much soul searching, I decided I couldn't part with my trumpet but the Nord needed to be played, so I'd have to find someone new to love it as much as I did.

I started compiling a list of what was to go and suddenly realised what would lessen the pain - I'd donate every penny raised to the fantastic Parkinson's UK charity! It took on a new meaning then and gave me the incentive to push ahead.

My many musical friends helped out enormously and I am so grateful to them. 'Nordy' went to live up north with someone far more talented than me - I was so relieved he had a new home where he'd be loved, cared for, and played plenty.

17. TAKING STOCK

Taking stock eighteen months on from diagnosis there seemed to be so many things to say. However, in many ways there was also really nothing to say, in that life just goes on and you deal with your lot as best you can.

Returning to my first statement though, I was trying to put all my thoughts into some semblance of order and pick out what really mattered and what didn't, how the disease had or hadn't progressed, and what I'd learned on this journey so far.

Getting the medical stuff over with first, has my PD progressed? I'm only guessing I've come off lightly with my progression of the disease compared to some. The increasing lack of ability of my right hand to carry out fine motor skills like writing, typing, eating, etc., has been minimised by my heroic left hand's mostly sub-conscious efforts to take over so there is very little I can't do. 'Yet!' I hear seasoned parkies screaming. Thank you left hand - may the curse of PD escape you for as long as possible! I am trying not to think about the fact that long term more likely than not the tremor will spread to my left side and how on earth I'm going to do things then I really don't know. No point worrying about that now though, I'll cross that bridge when I come to it.

Walking is pretty much top of the list of Parkinson's difficulties. I'm sure no-one believes me as I still look reasonably normal and fit, but I'm becoming a great advocate of hidden disabilities. There are days when I am blue badge material despite looking fit and healthy - the pain and effort to walk just a short distance are enormous. Just because I'm not visibly crippled, bandaged, supported by sticks or crutches and my gait looks reasonably normal, twenty yards can be a big challenge.

My Blue Badge in its funky spotted cover!

The unpredictability and extent of variation in the severity of symptoms have surprised me. I have days when I feel almost normal and others when I am very close to attaching the label 'disabled' to myself. Some days I'm just too knackered to even think about it!

I am finding it a little easier to ask strangers for help and somewhat more confident about focusing on myself rather than worrying about holding people up or what they'll think. I do still want to wear a sandwich board saying 'I have Parkinson's' to save having to explain myself for whatever reason I may have caught someone's attention. With very few exceptions though people are accepting, sympathetic, and kind.

I recently got myself a sunflower lanyard, but I have yet to wear it. The Sunflower Lanyard scheme is relatively new and is aimed at alerting people to the fact that you have a hidden disability or brain injury and might need assistance. I mostly have someone with me so haven't felt I need it yet, but I'm a little sceptical as to whether enough people know about it for it to be effective. Anyone I've asked hasn't heard of it, but I think it's a great idea so please spread the word!

Life at this stage is fairly normal except that in general things take twice as long to do than they should and leave me twice as exhausted. I guess it's because even when parkies are relaxing their body isn't because the stiffness and tremor never really go away.

It must be so hard for 'normal' people to understand. The best thing I can think of for a non-parky to emulate it, is trying to keep your fist clenched all the time or your arm flexed solid when you walk and see how tired and uncomfortable you get. Or imagine walking and suddenly you stand on some superglue and your leg just won't move - that's the freezing thing that gets us when we're least expecting it. Thankfully, my leg doesn't do that ... yet.

'Yet' is the ominous word that hangs over parkies all the time and torments us if we let it. Parkinson's Disease is different for everyone and you just don't know which of the array of not-so-nice symptoms are waiting to creep up on you. I won't list them just now or I'll get writers' cramp but do Google them sometime - it'll certainly make you count your blessings!

There is one super annoying thing that occurred to me. Since the stiffness and tremor mean my body never really stops, why isn't it using up heaps of calories and making me a nice neat size 10 rather than the baby hippopotamus I have become? At least there would be one perk!

Weight inevitably brings me back to the subject of exercise. My neuro pilates class is a godsend at keeping my core flexible and strong but I'm still failing to resurrect my running and much-needed cardio. I just can't seem to accept that I'm not able to do it, because in some strange way on the treadmill it often feels as though it's easier to run than walk, but I'm not able to sustain it for any length of time as however hard I try I can't get into a rhythm. I'm sure my excess couple of stones aren't helping either so it's a complete catch 22.

Thank goodness for the various online forums and Facebook groups I have access to as they are my only source of information and support. The UK based one 'Purely Parkinson's' on Facebook is particularly good - informative, amusing, and well moderated – but maybe I'm biased because I am one of the admins! Being fair though, the reason I ended up taking on that role is because it was my favourite site for parky chat. Of course, those run by Parkinson's UK and Parkinson's UK in Scotland are excellent sources of news, views, and research updates.

I'd had zero input from the neurology services and to be honest by this stage - late 2018 - I was getting a bit pissed-off! The promised appointment one year after diagnosis never appeared and I'd not heard a squeak from the Parkinson's nurses, I didn't even know if I had one now that the original lady had retired - mind you, she was as much use as a chocolate firework. Yes, I'm still annoyed with her for sending me a pile of completely inappropriate leaflets for my stage of the disease.

I'd soon be heading for two years since diagnosis at this rate. Once more Parkinson's really felt like the forgotten disease.

18. LOSING FAITH

One thing the wonderful charity Parkinson's UK is especially good at is constantly canvassing the opinion of people with the disease, their carers, and others involved with this 'select' group of people. They don't just cover a topic once then move on to another one, but they re-visit things to keep tabs on the ever-changing situations and issues that can face us. I always try to fill these in as honestly as possible to do my little bit to help the charity remain as good as it is.

At the tail end of 2018 one popped up on Facebook about post-diagnosis care, so as always I completed it, pressed submit, and forgot about it.

Lo and behold they contacted me shortly after having read my answers, quite shocked that two years was fast approaching, and I'd had no follow-up at all. They asked me a few questions and offered to see if they could help. I was absolutely over the moon! Within two, that's 2, I mean TWO days, the neurologist's secretary phoned, and I had an appointment lined up. Absolutely fantastic, the day couldn't come soon enough!

PARKINSON'S^{UK}
SCOTLAND
CHANGE ATTITUDES.
FIND A CURE.
JOIN US.

Thanks a million Parkinson's UK!

© Parkinson's UK
Reproduced with kind permission of Parkinson's UK, a registered charity in England & Wales (258197) and in Scotland (SC037554)

Monday 14th January 2019

Back to the big hospital for the big appointment!

We were ushered in by the neurologist in the same non-conversational manner we remembered from diagnosis day, and he sat down... diagonally opposite us at the other end of the room. Hmmm... 'how odd' I thought... 'I must be wearing the wrong perfume or something.'

He began to speak, but so quietly I was struggling to hear him as he asked how I was. I began to explain but he didn't really seem to be listening particularly intently, so I felt a bit awkward and curtailed what I wanted to say.

He then took hold of my hands and told me to relax and let him move my wrists, asked me to do as fast a pincer movement as I could with the forefinger and thumb of each hand, made no comment then said, 'Well, the gold standard treatment for Parkinson's is still levodopa, it can be a life-changer, but it's up to you whether you want to take it or not. What do you ultimately want to be able to do?'.

I wasn't quite sure what he meant by that question, but I explained that more than anything I wanted to be able to exercise effectively and maybe even run again. I think that was the wrong answer because he looked at me oddly and reiterated that the choice of whether to start on some drugs had to be mine. I turned to my husband for help and he voiced what I think I was trying to articulate. 'I think if the drugs mean that, apart from anything else, you'll be able to exercise again then I think that's worth it.'.

I asked the consultant about side effects as I'd read some awful things, but he just said they should be minimised by properly managing the dosage.

'Ok, I'll go for it.' I said, and that was it, there was no further discussion. A letter was to be written to my GP and he'd issue a prescription. Fifteen minutes tops in and out.

The only word I could use to describe the way I felt afterwards was 'blank'. Starting drugs was such a big deal for me, I felt it would change the whole dynamic of my Parkinson's, but the appointment had turned out to be such a non-event. And I could tell my husband was not happy either. Not good!

I turned to the only place I knew I could get help, the online community via my blog.

Take the drugs my friend you've held off long enough. It'll get you out running (hopefully) and you'll then get the dreaded weight off. 😊

1y   Like   Reply   ○3

I am in same place. Thank you for sharing your dilemma. I am anxious to read replies.

1y   Like   Reply

I think you will find the effects/damage that is being done to you by not taking the medications are far worse than taking the medications. Try looking at it this way....your body is asking for help.... the medication is the help that is needed.

1y   Like   Reply   ○3
      ○8

This is the question I really struggled with but I've spoken to a number of neurologists and PD nurses who have all said that the studies show there are no benefits to delaying taking the meds. The way it's been explained to me is that it's best to take the minimum amount you need to enable you to live well, exercise well etc. That's the best way to keep PD at bay for as long as possible.

If your PD symptoms are impacting your daily life (ie ... ...ing) I would take th... s VERY impo...

I was very reluctant to start on levadopa (the thinking at the time was that you only get limited years and as a relative pup the later the better.) I also never would take a headache pill. At the end of the day the meds are friends not foes. Go with and enjoy the benefits..   ○4

1y   Like   Reply

Having moved hesitantly from no medication to the medication in which my neurologist had led me to have high hopes, after about nine weeks things were turning out to be a complete damp squib. The tremor was perhaps a little better but the main target, the rigidity, just the same. No hint of pain-free walking and certainly no longed for running.

The lack of response to the drugs was really hard to deal with. I had been so excited at the prospect of all the things they might open the door to again.

My husband and I were also harbouring a growing feeling of resentment towards the neurologist. The twice we had seen him we both felt he had shown little interest or empathy, and his advice was minimal, to say the least. He had never asked me about the multitude of non-motor symptoms that can come with Parkinson's, he had never asked me a single thing about my lifestyle or work situation, there had been no mention of exercise and not a scrap of advice about how to take the drugs he was prescribing or some of the extremely serious side effects they can pose. The fact that he was the double of Dobby in the Harry Potter movies possibly wasn't helping our confidence in him either, but it did at least give us something to laugh about!

However, I decided it was all part of a learning curve, and rather than get upset I needed to teach myself to man up.

And that I did. To say I went to the six-month follow-up appointment prepared would be an understatement. I was simply not going to accept his 'just take the tablets' approach. I'd had enough and I think he knew by my demeanour when I walked in, as my husband said afterwards that poor Dobby looked a little intimidated!

I started by going right back to the beginning and asked to see my scans and have a full explanation of them. He was more than a little flustered. I did actually slightly shoot myself in the foot there as they were worse than

I'd expected, but I ploughed on all the same. I took him into territory he clearly wasn't expecting.

'In light of the fact that I have not responded to these drugs how certain can you be that I actually have Parkinson's Disease and not another Parkinsonian disorder?' I said forthrightly.

By these, I meant things like Cortico Basal Degeneration and Multiple System Atrophy, etc., which can initially manifest themselves similarly to Parkinson's Disease but are not the actual disease itself. He admitted that was a possibility, which I didn't really want to hear as they make Parkinson's itself look like a walk in the park in comparison, but I guess I did ask.

Seriously, you really don't want to Google those diseases - they don't make for pleasant reading. I quizzed him about other drug options, deep brain stimulation surgery, more information on side effects, what the next course of action would be if the doubling of my dosage that he was suggesting didn't work, and so it went on. I extracted every bit of information out of him that I could, he answered but he still never offered anything or said more than the bare minimum.

I'm not sure who was more exhausted by the end, me or him! I felt satisfied that at least I was a bit better informed, but I knew this man totally didn't have my back and I was somehow going to have to find someone else to guide me on my journey.

19. TAKING CONTROL

It was now mid-2019 and I was shovelling in four times my original dose of medication daily as per Dobby-the-Neurologist's instruction, going to my neuro pilates class, and riding my e-bike. But I didn't feel like I had any clear direction or medical support. Everything I knew about Parkinson's I'd had to find out myself and I now also had a question mark hanging over me as to whether I actually had PD or one of its nasty neighbours. There were no further appointments lined up. Was this it? Was I just going to bumble on now until something dramatic happened, or keep taking more and more tablets the further down the hill I slid?

For many people that would have probably been fine, but not for me. I'm not sure whether it's a good trait or a bad trait, but I am just not able to sit back and let things happen. I always feel I ought to be doing something to help myself – I like to have a plan. I know I'm certainly guilty of thinking too much – those who know me well run for cover when I start a sentence with the words 'I've been thinking…'!

Cogito, ergo sum.
I think, therefore I am.

I took to the Internet. I wanted to find out who the leading lights in Parkinson's in my part of the UK were and what the current 'talk on the street' about it was.

The names of two consultants in Scotland kept popping up as speakers at conferences and in media articles, so I made it my mission to find them and see one of them. They were both more than a hundred miles away but no pain, no gain. A bit more digging and I discovered that one of them luckily consulted privately – perfect. I cherish our NHS, but I felt it was letting me down badly, so 'desperate times desperate measures' and I am lucky enough that I can afford to pay for a private appointment, so I booked myself in.

He was my big hope - hope that I had found someone who would take an interest in me as an individual rather than 'another case of Parkinson's Disease', someone I could relate to and would relate to me, and someone who would have a plan and get me moving forward again from the limbo I was in.

With the lack of support from anywhere, I had been relying heavily on my two fantastic private physiotherapists whose understanding, support, and knowledge had, in all honesty, been my lifeline. They both knew me extremely well by this time and could sense my frustration, so while I was waiting for my private neurology appointment they came up with a plan. They encouraged me to join a gym, and together they took me around and devised a personalised parky exercise circuit - just for me! It was absolutely brilliant and gave me a much-needed new focus. I even treated myself to a new marquee sized swimming costume and started swimming again too!

The days went by one by one with each bringing its own set of physical and/or mental challenges the way that Parkinson's inevitably does, but I could feel the benefits of the gym as my number of repetitions increased or I'd add another weight on to the machine. Every step forward seemed to bring with it a step back though, but I ploughed on feeling at least I was trying my best to make my situation better rather than sit back and rely on drugs to do the job for me. The high of swimming 50 lengths of the pool would turn into a low of headaches and fatigue... a fun game of table tennis (supposed to be very good for Parkinson's) would set off a new set of leg and foot pain. But whatever ache or injury I presented my fab physios with, they worked through it with me and put me back on the road again and again. They really were my absolute rocks. If I had one piece of advice to give a fledgling parky it would be get yourself a pair of damn good physios.

😎 PHYSIOTHERAPIST WORSHIP 🖤

Although I loved my gym sessions from the get-go, there is no doubt you need to develop a thick skin with Parkinson's. The last time I'd been in a gym I was a svelte size 10 that hardly broke sweat sprinting on the treadmill for thirty minutes, before lifting serious amounts of weight for someone a whisker bigger than five feet. It took more than a little courage to make my return to the gym as a large, stiff, clumsy, heifer like creature with the wobbles! I wanted some sort of announcement over the tannoy to say:

> *The person about to enter the gym is not a lazy blob and only resembles a hippopotamus because she has a heart condition and Parkinson's!*

Sadly that wasn't going to happen so I resorted to collecting together an array of Cure Parkinson's Trust and Parkinson's UK t-shirts to wear for my

workouts in the hope they might offer some explanation to fellow gym users as to my sad physical state. Isn't it completely pathetic that I felt I needed to do that? Probably nobody else gave a damn and I was just being completely vain, but it's the sad truth. As it turned out over time, there were a lot more interesting sights than me!

The gym I'd joined wasn't one of those massive things with banks of treadmills in rows and scores of muscle men pumping iron - it was the gym belonging to a rather upmarket country club type place. This was chosen because it was close by, quiet, had a good range of facilities, and also so that my husband could use the driving range and nine-hole golf course if he didn't feel like joining his walrus of a wife splashing her way up and down the pool or clumping around the gym. (It also happened to be where we'd held our wedding reception quarter of a century earlier.).

Anyway, any thoughts of being self-conscious about my appearance were dispelled when one day I was sweating my way through the French Alps on a rather fancy exercise bike when in sailed an extremely well-dressed lady in a cloud of expensive perfume. Her hair was perfectly coiffed, she was wearing an expensive-looking coordinated 'leisure outfit' that looked like it had come from one of those extortionate little boutiques that only stock one of each size - all 'accessorised' by much ostentatious gold jewellery and a black snakeskin looking bag hanging from a gold chain strap on her shoulder.

She glanced around with a look of disdain that there were other 'beings' polluting her space, then swept towards one of the treadmills. Out of the snakeskin bag appeared a box of delicately perfumed wipes - well, I couldn't actually smell them but I bet they were - and she painstakingly cleaned away any trace of germs that may have been left by a previous 'unclean' occupant. (This was long before Covid 19). She then quickly checked her hair and make-up in her mirror compact, switched on the treadmill, and embarked upon a gentle stroll with her head held high, her back ramrod straight - and her shoulder bag still on!

It took every ounce of my willpower not to fall off the exercise bike laughing! It was as though she was demonstrating a lesson in deportment at a posh Swiss finishing school.

Ten minutes later she gracefully stepped off and left with not a hair out of place nor a bead of sweat.

I looked around the room and it seemed that while I was glued to this vision before me, not one other person had remotely noticed. Well if that hadn't halted their kettle balls in full swing perhaps my rotund presence wouldn't either – excellent!

I'd pay good money for CCTV footage of the whole performance – it still makes me chuckle.

20. ON THE ROAD

Tuesday 17th September 2019

Heading south for my private appointment I was filled with anticipation. Surely it had to be better, simply from the fact that this neurologist was a Parkinson's specialist unlike Dobby, whose specialism (apart from having less bedside manner than I have dopamine left in my brain) was another non-movement neurological issue.

I've only ever been to a private hospital once before in my life and wasn't particularly impressed. It was a large old building that had been extended so many times it was a warren of slightly shabby carpeted hallways and staircases that seemed pretty unfit for purpose. This one had a reasonably impressive reception area but was of a similar ilk as soon as you got past that. Checking in was a stark reminder of how lucky we are to have our NHS when they took my credit card details, reminded me of any add-on-costs, and handed me a receipted invoice. It felt so strange dealing with money for a medical appointment.

Needless to say, true to form we were incredibly early so went in search of a café to fill some time and our bellies. In a private hospital, the eatery was bound to be rather nice surely? It had been a long journey and I was looking forward to something along the lines of a freshly brewed pot of coffee with a fancy cup and saucer (certainly not my norm), and a tray of delicate little sandwiches with their crusts cut off, decorated with a sprig of parsley (definitely not my norm either). One would expect table-service as well of course.

What we were greeted with was an enormously high unwelcoming barren room with a selection of sorry looking vending machines - petrol station like coffee in a paper cup and a packet of crisps. How disappointed can you be?

Somewhat deflated we didn't hang around in there and went to navigate our way to the correct waiting room on the top floor via a rather strange lift system. It took us up two floors, made us disembark, walk a few metres to another minuscule lift which went the rest of the way and opened directly into the waiting room itself. The second lift was so small it was like being delivered in a space capsule.

Judging by the remnants of a rather fine ceiling cornice, in its heyday this must have been quite an impressive building. It certainly wasn't any longer and it didn't remotely feel like a hospital. There was no hustle and bustle like the NHS, in fact, it was so incredibly quiet it almost felt like the staff were actively avoiding making any noise. 'What an awful place to work.' I thought.

We were eventually called through by a very smiley young-ish (well, 40ish is young in my book) consultant, whose demeanour was already entirely different from Dobby's. I knew he was going to want to know why I had come all the way to see him rather than go to my local NHS neurologist, so I had a carefully thought out diplomatic answer up my sleeve. I may not have liked Dobby and privately thought he was completely useless, but I didn't want to be rude or critical - I just don't think it's necessary or appropriate to be unpleasant - so I explained that I felt the service in my home town was extremely stretched so I'd had very little input and that the person I saw was not a PD specialist and we didn't really 'gel'.

He seemed to accept that without raising an eyebrow and started his investigations. He had me walking watching my gait, gave me balance tests, talked about non-motor symptoms, treatment options, and side effects, all whilst taking copious notes.

There was so much I found myself saying that I'd never said before because nobody had asked. It felt like a very productive 45 minutes and I was buzzing! Not only did we have a plan to move forward starting with a new additional drug to try, but he'd ruled out the worry of me having one of those horrid Parkinson's related diseases like Cortico Basal Degeneration or Multiple System Atrophy. He even told me what type of Parkinson's he reckoned I may have - Benign Tremulous Parkinsonism. That was a completely new one on me, I'd never heard of it before. It explained why I don't seem to have a typical resting tremor but can have it quite fiercely during activity too, and it is also characterised by a poor response to the levodopa medicine - which I had. At last - a proper name for my 'Stubborn Parkinson's Syndrome' as I'd nicknamed it.

The other good thing is that apparently BTP (I don't know if that's an official abbreviation, but it's far too long to keep saying) doesn't generally progress as fast as other types of PD and remains relatively contained to your tremoring area. There is also a reasonably successful surgical option called deep brain stimulation (officially this time known as DBS), but that would be a long way off and I'm not sure if it would be compatible with my implantable cardioverter defibrillator. It involves attaching electrodes deep in the brain, which are then linked to a kind of brain pacemaker that sends signals that over-ride the tremor. Perhaps the two electrical devices might cause interference with each other - that could be awkward! I wonder if anyone else has ever had both? With those plus my metal ankle, there is no way I would get through airport security!

He sent me off with an instruction to try out a new additional medication in the form of a sticky patch and re-book to see him in three months.

It had been a long, tiring, and expensive day, but so worth it. I felt back in control with a renewed sense of direction, and also vindicated in my feeling that the appointments I had had so far fell well short of the mark. I knew for sure that I wouldn't be going back to see Dobby again.

Sorry NHS, but you let me down big style on this occasion – I do still cherish you though.

21. STICKY SITUATION

I was very excited about my new parky medicated patches but had to patiently wait for a whole two weeks, which isn't long at all but felt like it, until the neurologist's letter had reached my GP and the poor over-burdened GP had got round to reading it and writing the prescription.

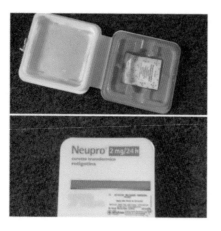

The package I picked up from the pharmacy was huge and had me wondering where on earth I was going to stick this seemingly rather large 6 inch square! As it turned out they were actually only about a 2cm square, but came in a super fancy box which opened like a book with the little things all neatly protected in the middle surrounded by plastic. Talk about over packaging!

I had been warned that I'd have to start on a very small dose and work up to the neurologist's suggested level as it lessened the chance of any unpleasant side effects, so I thought I better check them out so I knew exactly what to be prepared for.

Oh my goodness - it was like reading the script for an 18-rated psychological thriller:

- *Severe allergic reactions that may be life-threatening*
- *Suddenly falling asleep without warning while doing normal activities such as driving a car*
- *Hallucinations and other psychosis - excessive suspicion, aggressive behaviour, delusional beliefs*
- *Unusual urges - increased sexual urges and behaviours (oh my, how embarrassing!), unusual urges to gamble or spend money*
- *Uncontrolled sudden movements*

Those in addition to the run of the mill nausea, vomiting, headaches, dizziness, fainting, lowered blood pressure, increased sweating, vision problems, leg swelling, rashes, itching, etc.

It was hard to believe that such an innocent-looking little sticking plaster could harbour such a house of horrors!

Five days in and all was good. They were pulling my leg, this was a pussy cat of a plaster! No skin reaction, no nausea, no hallucinations, no compulsive gambling, or spending. I did have a day of hiccups, which surprisingly is actually listed as a side effect in some places! I found it rather amusing at first but less so by the fourth hour-long bout.

Day 6 and I had the mother of all headaches and was quite light-headed, but I was going to give my wee plaster-friend the benefit of the doubt as you can sometimes get a general crappy parky day rather than a patch-induced crappy parky day. I was also learning that the plaster stays on better if I stick it to less flabby bits of me, of which there are fewer than I like to admit.

I was becoming quite fond of my little patches if I'm honest, so was really hoping they'd work - they somehow felt less like taking medicine than tablets do.

By week 5, having stepped up a dose I was still doing ok, but something in the patient leaflet was both niggling and slightly amusing me! It warns that if you are to receive cardioversion (electric shock on your heart) you must remove your patch first as it contains aluminium and can burn. So, I pondered, if my implantable cardioverter defibrillator for my genetic heart condition were to shock me, would the bit where I'm wearing the patch blow up or ignite?! Secondly, if I'm in the position of needing cardioversion I'm guessing removing my patch is not going to be top of my list of priorities - I would have thought that staying alive to see another day might be more pressing!

As it happens, I had a routine cardiology check-up so asked the question: the electro-physiologist, clearly trying to keep a straight face, answered in all seriousness and basically affirmed my theory that surviving takes priority over burning. That's handy to know!

I was standing in a queue at the checkout of our local convenience store one day, and the man behind me said, 'I've got one of them too, nightmare isn't it?'

I hadn't the faintest idea what he was talking about. 'I'm sorry?' I said looking at him quizzically.

He nodded towards the patch on my arm, 'How are you getting on with them?'

'Oh my' I thought, 'someone else with Parkinson's,' and replied, 'Not bad so far thanks, but I've not being using them very long. I think maybe the tremor is a little better though.'

He did a sharp intake of breath, shook his head and said 'You must have smoked a lot then? I was on 30 a day but I'm down to about 10 now.'

The penny dropped. Hilarious - he thought it was a nicotine patch!

I just smiled and said, 'Yeah, but I'll get there. Good luck.'

It just wasn't worth trying to explain!

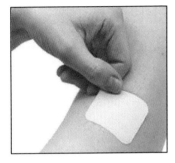 As time went on, and I very gradually crept up the dosage ladder, it seemed to be an increasing combination of highs and lows. When it worked it worked so well I was like a spring chicken and felt cured! I wanted to swing my arms around wildly and dance naked in the rain - and it was the best feeling in the world getting a glimpse of how smoothly and easily my body used to function. (I didn't use to do the dancing naked in the rain thing by the way.)

On occasions, I could also smell better too, by that I mean my sense of smell improved. Poor sense of smell is a non-motor PD symptom - who knows whether I actually smelled better! I also hadn't had any more bouts of serial hiccupping.

However, I started to have weird dreams and weird feelings and sometimes felt generally weird in the head. I had an entire night of being tormented by the word 'unhinged'. I felt it and could see it, and wanted to tell the world it – shout it out in the street!

Thankfully, I wasn't whacky enough to not realise that this was the drug messing with my brain. There was also a feeling of slight anxiety creeping in, of which I immediately became very wary, plus regular bad indigestion and strange feelings towards some foods I normally like. All very odd.

I was starting to wonder whether sadly my little magic patches weren't going to be quite so magical after all. I really wanted them to work so being the eternal optimist I carried on. I mean, in the grand scale of things, according to the horror movie patient leaflet, it could be a whole lot worse. There really should be a warning leaflet for that warning leaflet.

Periodically throughout this journey I try to be realistic with myself and ask myself these three questions:

Is it hard? Yes, it's bloody hard.
Can I keep fighting? Yes, no question - I have to.
Is life still good? Yes - life is still good.
The answer to the last two was still 'yes', so onwards and upwards!

Or maybe not! Thereafter followed a horrendous onslaught of dizziness, nausea, vomiting, and an altogether supreme level of utter crappiness (personal technical term).

I called the Parkinson's nurse service for help. She said to step down the dose immediately, but unfortunately somewhere en-route her message via the practice pharmacist to the local chemist to reduce the strength got confused and my new batch of patches turned out to still be the higher strength.

I had been warned not to come straight off them altogether under any circumstances, but I couldn't bear the thought of more 'patch-poisoning' while the prescription was sorted out, so I came up with a cunning plan!

Reading all the literature it seemed that the patches got bigger in size as the dosages increased, and according to my sums every $10cm^2$ corresponded to a 2mg per 24 hours dosage of Rotigotine. My current 6mg one was $30cm^2$, but I needed to drop to 4mg - so I simply chopped a third of it off! Was that really naughty? I had this nagging feeling that I'd read somewhere not to do that but maybe that was just my guilty conscience.

Perhaps an infuriated pharmacist would come after me? In my defence, I figured that every third day I could stick on all the chopped off bits to make up a whole patch again - waste not want not. Perhaps I'd get struck off for being a rebel patch cutter.

Sadly, despite my illicit patch-pruning and then some officially lower dose ones, I continued to be super sick. I lasted another five weeks vomiting and feeling generally dreadful then made an appointment to see the GP. A lovely nurse practitioner listened to my tale of woe but said I just had to keep slowly reducing the dosage, however, drinking apple juice would ease my now extremely irritated stomach and help replace electrolytes lost from the vomiting. We went and cleared the local supermarket shelf of cartons!

Following an extensive non-clinical trial, I can exclusively reveal that drinking apple juice to alleviate nausea and vomiting is a load of tosh. If nothing else, it tastes slightly less vile than the rest of the contents of your stomach when they come back up again... and again... and again...

Hmmm, what to do with the remaining five thousand cartons...

22. SICK AS A DOG

As I slowly stepped down the dosage of my killer patches, I had also been starting to feel that I could perhaps be better managing my levodopa medication. I was taking 200mg three times a day at 9am, 3pm and 9pm - but seemed to find that I became stiff and useless early evening. I wondered about splitting the 9pm dose and taking half (100mg) earlier to get some benefit during the evening rather than all the effect coming at night when I was in bed and didn't really need it.

Having made contact with the Parkinson's nurse service over my patches and got a friendly, helpful response, I called and left a message again.

Oh dear! Different PD nurse, different response. Severe ticking off. No way was I to do that as there would be so many hours here, which would leave so many hours there, and that would be completely out of the question. It was as though I'd suggested sticking the capsules up my nose or feeding them to the cat! I slunk off the telephone with my tail between my legs.

The more I thought about it the more annoyed I got, so once more I turned to my online parky pals for reassurance that I hadn't made a stupid suggestion and wasn't being touchy feeling aggrieved by the response.

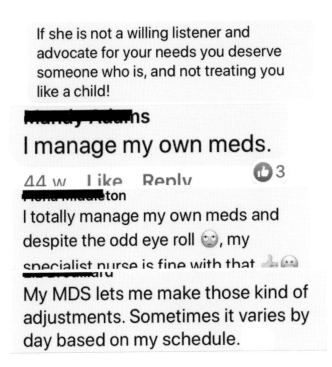

If she is not a willing listener and advocate for your needs you deserve someone who is, and not treating you like a child!

ns

I manage my own meds.

44 w   Like   Reply   👍 3

ton

I totally manage my own meds and despite the odd eye roll 🙄, my specialist nurse is fine with that 👍😫

My MDS lets me make those kind of adjustments. Sometimes it varies by day based on my schedule.

They wholeheartedly supported my reasons for wanting to alter the dosage the way I'd suggested. Phew - at least I knew I hadn't been barking up the wrong tree, but it continued to irk me. I know we all have bad days and get tetchy, but it wasn't as though I'd caught her at a bad moment. I had left a message and she had called me back presumably at a time that was convenient to her? So why the negative attitude? Now call me cynical but I couldn't help wondering - it surely wouldn't be because I went 'private' looking for a neurologist who'd listen - would it? Surely not?

The answer I will never know, but thankfully a different Parkinson's nurse called me a few days later out of the blue to make an appointment to come to see me at home. I was delighted! We set a date and before hanging up I quickly snuck in a second stab at my question about splitting the evening dose of my medication.

'Oh yes,' she said, 'Absolutely fine - if you think that might suit you better by all means go ahead. As long as there's no significant change in the overall daily dosage, you distribute them throughout the day the way you think best.'

Well, blow me down with a feather - sometimes I just don't get it!

Anyway, along she came to the house for a visit mid-November 2019. She was a nice friendly lady around my age and seemed to have been a PD nurse for a long time, so would have seen it all. I was running through a very potted version of my history with her, getting increasingly uncomfortable, knowing the bit about dispensing with Dobby's services in favour of the private consultant was coming up.

When I sheepishly admitted it, she said, sounding quite unconcerned, 'Yes, I saw the private consultant's letter in your notes.', and for a fleeting moment I thought I'd got away with it.

But no, she then dropped in, 'Of course, there's nothing he could do that we can't do here, but if you want to spend money on it that's your choice.'

However, in her defence, she was then extremely understanding when I explained that I didn't seem to get on with Dobby and that I was really embarrassed to ask, but was there any way of moving consultant?

'It's probably my fault.' I said not wanting to cause any ill-feeling, 'I hope I'm not putting you in an awkward position.' I bumbled on.

To her credit, she was very reassuring, telling me that she totally understood and saying that these things happen.

Then she suddenly exclaimed 'Oh, wait a minute, I've had an idea, I know exactly what I'll do!'

She told me a new consultant had just been appointed and was starting in the New Year. She knew him well as he'd been a clinical lecturer for a number of years previously and had done a lot of research into PD. She reckoned he would be perfect for me, especially as he was quite young so hopefully would be around for a while to give continuity of care. She promised to speak to him and get back to me. It sounded really promising but I was scared to build up my hopes.

The rest of the appointment was fairly uneventful, and we talked about many things out with Parkinson's Disease including a mutual friend it turned out we had - a small world once again! I didn't really learn anything more Parkinson's related, but it had been worth it just to get the chance of a new NHS consultant locally.

Despite her helpfulness, I have to say I got the feeling she didn't really like me, but she has every right not to so that's not a criticism, just an observation. Not that it's of much consequence – liking me is not mandatory and I can be very annoying! I mentioned it to my husband, but he hadn't picked up on it. Perhaps I was being a bit paranoid.

Mind you if anyone should be paranoid it should be him. He dutifully drives me to all my appointments these days and comes in with me to each consultation. Then if any nurses, doctors, or similar come to the house, he acts as a butler bringing us teas and coffees, laying out biscuits and offering top-ups, etc., so we can get on with our meeting. And for all that the poor thing gets summarily ignored. Health professionals pay him virtually no notice. Their conversation is always entirely directed at me and they have hardly ever made any attempt to engage with him.

I find this very odd and even more so, a missed opportunity. He has, through no choice of his own, had the job of carer foisted upon him whether he likes it or not. Admittedly, I'm not really at the stage of needing 'care' as such but he is the one and only person who ever sees the full extent of my Parkinson's Disease and witnesses first-hand the ups and downs. He has known me longer than anyone and knows what I was like before, so if anyone actually took the time to ask, I think he'd have some extremely valuable input.

The spouse of anyone with a degenerative medical condition has a huge burden dropped upon them and for no health professional to even say 'How are you coping?' or 'How do you feel?' is disappointing.

23. THE ROLLERCOASTER

There is a particularly important phenomenon in Parkinson's that I must explain as it is literally central to our existence, for most of us anyway. Non-parkies generally don't know about it and to an onlooker, it can appear at best amazing, at worst unbelievable, to the point where people might even think we are having them on.

It is the ON/OFF effect of the main drug that most of us take - levodopa. It is actually officially called ON and OFF, that isn't a lay term or one I've made up, named so because it is exactly that - ON being when the drug is working and OFF being when it's not.

In very basic terms, Parkinson's is a lack of dopamine in our brains and dopamine controls our movement. Levodopa temporarily replaces that missing dopamine, so when it's in our system we are ON and can move much better and more smoothly - when it's not we are OFF and can't. Different people get it to a different extent of course, but as my disease progresses, I notice my ONs and OFFs are becoming far more marked.

The secret to combatting ONs and OFFs is a finely tuned daily drugs juggling act. In the earlier days of taking the drugs, I was able to take them reasonably regularly spaced out during the day and the effect was fairly constant, but as I deteriorate it is becoming more of a rollercoaster as they don't last all day and I'm already on a fairly high dose so don't want to increase it unless I absolutely have to.

Things are easier if you have a reasonably regular routine, it's when you don't that the real juggling begins. You need to think ahead as to when you want to be at your most functional. Say I'm meeting someone for coffee at 11am, I really want my morning tablet to be peaking between say 11 & 12.30. Normally it would be starting to wear off towards the end of that 'window' so that day I'd probably take it a little later in the morning than usual. However, if the meeting is for lunch at 1pm (and I want to be able to eat and cut my own food with reasonable ease!) that's a different ball game. I can't drag out my morning tablet till then, but the afternoon one usually hasn't kicked in fully by 1pm, so I need to shunt them along accordingly - the morning one early so I can take the second one a little earlier too.

If you think that's all a bit of a pain in the neck, add to it the hurdle that the tablets can be badly affected by eating protein too close to when you take them.

So, in actual fact you're juggling three balls:
1. *When you take the tablet for peak effect*
2. *When you eat to fit in with that*
3. *What you eat when you do eat!*

Again, the protein effect varies from person to person and I'm not too bad on this front yet - but I have noticed that if for example, I drink a large glass of milk before my tablets their effect is considerably reduced.

A further fly in the ointment is that you also need to be careful that in your eagerness to make sure you're functional for a particular time, that you don't overlap the doses. Too much medication can cause things called dystonia and dyskinesia, which are when you get involuntary movements of your muscles. If you have perhaps seen the most famous Parkinson's sufferer of all time, Michael J. Fox, in recent years, you'll have noticed the kind of squirming his body does.

Now, you might understandably be thinking, does this ON/OFF thing really make that much difference? Believe me, it does. It is one of the key difficulties for Parkinson's sufferers to the point where it can have a serious effect on their life rather than just being inconvenient or embarrassing.

For me, an OFF can mean tremoring so much my right hand and arm are virtually unusable. They are rigid and painful with muscle spasms that can also lead to horrible headaches. If I'm really bad my teeth can chatter and I get a hideous internal tremor which is extremely unnerving. I have to take stairs one by one going down when I'm OFF and when I walk my right foot twists and drags making as short a distance as going between rooms in the house an effort. Those parkies with more advanced disease may not even be able to walk properly at all, just shuffle. However, when I'm ON, for example, I can clean the kitchen with both hands, even write fairly well with my right hand. I can use knives and forks reasonably normally, walk downstairs normally and even play table tennis and badminton! I am a different person. You would be forgiven for thinking I'm 'at it' when I'm OFF.

Sadly, so little about this phenomenon is understood by so many people in positions in which they should know better, it can have disastrous repercussions for many parkies. One of the main ones I read so much about is medical assessments for things like disability benefits, blue badges, bus passes, etc. You need to take your medication if you want to have any hope of being able to get to the assessment, but you can't just switch off the effect when you arrive to reveal your 'raw' state. The assessors see either a completely false you, or they think as long as you just keep taking the tablets, you'll always be fine. They do not realise that in any one day you can literally swing ON & OFF two or three times between being able-bodied and quite considerably disabled.

This of course brings me back to my hidden disabilities thing. I might have a blue badge and look fine to an onlooker. Look at me again in an hour and you may see something completely different.

There are other forms of levodopa than the usual capsules, and also additional drugs that can help iron out the ON/OFF fluctuations, but for many, they remain a constant issue.

Another little hitch worth mentioning are those 'lovely' days when the blessed levodopa tablets would be as well being jellybeans! For no explicable reason, they just don't work. It doesn't matter whether I've eaten or not eaten protein, or what time I've taken the infernal things, they just decide not to do a damn thing!

Parkinson's 1, Me 0.

There is but only one solution - suck it up (moan a lot to any unfortunate person who happens to be within earshot, even the cat!) and remember that tomorrow is another day. Crappinson's will not beat me!

Yawn...yes Mum, I've heard it all before.....

24. THE BEST YET

Tuesday 28th January 2020

Time to meet my third neurologist! I have to admit to feeling a little sheepish whilst sitting in the waiting area in case Dobby was lurking around the out-patient clinic and spotted the evil rebel patient who'd rejected him. My eyes kept darting around the comings and goings but thankfully there was no sign of him.

We were greeted by an intelligent-looking young fellow who had with him my PD nurse and another PD nurse. I felt spoiled - all these people giving their time for me!

He had only been speaking for about five minutes and I was already feeling glad I'd taken the bull by the horns and asked to change to someone other than Dobby. I had felt genuinely bad doing that and found it embarrassing and uncomfortable, but this chap was a different kettle of fish altogether and I warmed to him immediately. Huge thanks to the Parkinson's nurse for organising the swap for me.

'New-Neurologist', apart from actually being a Parkinson's specialist, really probed and listened which was wonderful and such a change from you know who. What was particularly refreshing was that he explored with genuine interest all of me, my mind, and my whole body, not just the parky bits. At one point he even had my shoes and socks off looking at the metalwork in my ankle from when I'd broken it and it had become the catalyst to this journey really beginning.

He did various walking, balancing, and dexterity tests similar to those the private neurologist had done and also seemed to want to suss out my emotional and mental attitude towards the disease, which I think is hugely important with any chronic illness. My own feeling is that medical outcomes are very much influenced by whether you're a fighter or a quitter. I like to think I'm a fighter, but I guess we all hope we are.

I embarrassingly confessed to chopping down the size of my Rotigotine patches when the side effects were making me so ill. He didn't tell me off - just gave me his rather fetching (oops, did I say that?!) smile, chuckled, and said 'Well, just as well you've got the lower dose ones now.'.

We briefly discussed deep brain stimulation surgery, but he said he'd need to get to know me as a person and the individual characteristics of my illness far better before considering that. And for the first time of anyone I'd seen, he delved in detail into the vast murky underworld of the non-motor symptoms of Parkinson's. The list of these is pretty long and includes:

- *Fatigue*
- *Low blood pressure*
- *Bladder/bowel problems*
- *Restless legs*
- *Skin/sweating problems*
- *Sleep issues*
- *Eating/swallowing/saliva control*
- *Vivid dreams*
- *Shouting/lashing out in your sleep*
- *Speech/communication problems*
- *Eye problems*

- *Foot care issues*
- *Pain*
- *Mouth/dental issues*
- *Memory/thinking problems*
- *Dementia*
- *Depression*
- *Lack of sense of smell or taste.*

For me, fatigue and insomnia are by far the most troublesome, although I also have the joy of occasional restless legs, a pretty poor sense of smell, and sweating (although that may be a lady's 'time of life' thing!).

'Nice New Neurologist' was extremely sympathetic about my sleep issues - probably the first health professional to really show an interest in it and properly appreciate how debilitating it is, although my current GP is pretty good too. He recommended I try white light therapy which involves exposing yourself to a special bright light when you wake in the morning, to try to reset your body clock to wake up in the day, and encourage it to produce melatonin at night when it's needed to promote sleep. He also prescribed a melatonin supplement and directed me to an App called Sleepio. I couldn't wait to try them all!

From the medication point of view, he suggested concentrating the doses of levodopa into the day only so I get the best movement effects when I'm up and about rather than later at night when I don't need to be physically active. That was totally different from what I had initially been told about spreading them at equal intervals throughout my waking hours but seemed to make a lot of sense. He also thought it was worth adding a new drug called Rasagiline - a once-daily tablet that acts to slow down the breakdown of dopamine in your brain. However, with this came a stark warning to be on the lookout for any sign of the possible side effect of compulsive behaviour. Oh dear... My husband did point out that being the extremely canny Scot I am, compulsive spending would probably just bring me up to the normal spending level of the general population!

The other peculiarity of Rasagiline is that you need to be careful what you eat and avoid foods containing tyramine, including cured, fermented or air-dried meats or fish, aged cheeses, fermented cabbage, soybean products, and red wine and tap beer. They can cause a potentially lethal spike in blood pressure. Oh no! With 50% German heritage eating salami is in my genes!

New-Neurologist had given me a full hour of his time and I felt truly grateful. I had really liked the private neurologist, but New-Neurologist was my favourite! I felt I could laugh with him, which for me is especially important, and that he was on my side and open to exploring options. Dobby had somehow made me feel there wasn't much out there to help with Parkinson's, but New-Neurologist gave me confidence that he had plenty up his sleeve that we could try as things progressed. How lucky was I? At last, a neurologist on my doorstep that I felt confident was willing to try his best to support me wherever Crappinson's was going to take me. The value of that when you're on this mystery tour of an illness is immeasurable. NHS worship!

He asked when I wanted to see him again. My mind immediately thought 'Tomorrow', but I figured that would be a bit presumptuous, so I politely and a bit mischievously suggested, 'Next week please!.'

Another nice smile from him and he said, 'I'll see you in six months.'.

I am really looking forward to my next appointment - how many sleeps is that?

25. SHUT EYE

I couldn't wait to get home, order my 10,000 lumens white light lamp, download the Sleepio App, and try out the melatonin.

Sleep has been a major issue for me for longer than I can remember, probably even right back to my teens. Some Parkinson's experts maintain it can be one of the earliest signs of the disease - who knows. In fact, just the other day I read a new theory that it could even be part of the cause of Parkinson's Disease. The thinking on this is that apparently when we are sleeping our brain acts like a washing machine, washing out all the toxins that are harmful to it. The researchers believe that when you don't get enough sleep, a protein called Alpha Synuclein builds up and leads to the destruction of dopamine-producing neurons in your brain. That fiend Alpha-Synuclein seems to also play a part in my heart defect, which adds weight to my own completely non-scientific theory that the two conditions are related for me.

Anyway, I had always put my poor sleep down to the many years when I worked as a broadcast journalist in radio and TV and produced and presented early morning news bulletins. For some time I lived a fair distance away from the TV station and had to get up at 2.30am for a 4am start. That meant going to bed at 7pm. For one reason or another, the outside world still being awake and making a noise or someone phoning etc., my precious sleep was invariably interrupted. Then the weekend would come, and it was like getting on and off a plane from America, moving my body clock by around 6 hours. For some that's no bother – I have a friend who has been presenting the early morning news programme on BBC Radio Scotland for 12 years and is still like a spring-chicken. Unfortunately, because sleep didn't come easily to me the spring went well out of my chicken!

Now, thank goodness I am happily retired so don't have to contemplate a day's work absolutely shattered before I even start. Being wide awake in the middle of the night is not the torture it used to be, but it can still be soul-destroying. The annoying thing is, if it's 2pm in the afternoon it's a different story altogether - my body can switch off in a nanosecond just when I don't really want it to.

I am sure the vast majority of non-Parkinsonian people have experienced insomnia at some point in their lives, but it's a different ball game altogether when it's on an ongoing basis for literally decades. I cannot remember the last time I slept for 8 hours straight. Well, actually I can, it was after work about five years ago when a colleague introduced me to Jägerbombs one evening... but that's another story...

The problem with insomnia, and I mean serial insomnia not common or garden insomnia as in the odd night's wakefulness here or there, is that nobody but nobody other than a fellow serial insomniac can truly understand what it is like and how destructive it is.

The new theory about Alpha-Synuclein aside, sleep relies on various chemicals in our brains like melatonin, serotonin, dopamine, which are basically all the things that are up the creek in a parky head!

Some people count sheep, I find the thing that is most likely to help me drop off is reciting all the things I've tried but have failed.

Here goes...

Chamomile tea
Warm milk
Alcohol
'Sleep hygiene'
Reading a book
Listening to a book
Not reading a book
Not listening to a book
White noise
No noise
Relaxing music
Relaxing voice
Bird song
Running water sounds
Meditation stuff
Weighted blanket
Hot room
Cool room
Open window
Sleep Apps
White light therapy
Blue light therapy
Pyjamas on /off
Bedding on / off ...on/off....on/off....
Exercise - but not too late
Exercise – but not too early either
No naps
No caffeine
No thinking
No worrying
Bach remedies
Lavender
Magnesium
Every other vitamin, mineral, etc.

With renewed optimism thanks to New-Neurologist, I ordered a white light that was relatively inexpensive, and I also downloaded the Sleepio App. Then a week later I picked up the melatonin supplement prescription.

I'd read a fair bit about white light in the past concerning sleep and mood etc., so was quite hopeful of a positive effect from that. I can't say I really enjoy sitting next to it first thing in the morning, but it is great for putting on my mascara. At least if it doesn't turn out to help my slumber in the long term, I've gained a really good make-up lamp!

The Sleepio App was interesting, and I like the fact that they've used a nice Scottish accent for the voiceover. Believe me, there are plenty of Scottish accents that certainly would not put you to sleep!

First of all, Sleepio has you keeping a note of your sleeping and waking hours to work out a thing called 'sleep efficiency'. Mine turned out to be extremely inefficient to say the least, surprise surprise. Then after a couple of weeks, it asks you not to go to bed until just before you intended to sleep. That doesn't really work for me as a parky, as I find it helps enormously to go and lie down on the bed in the evening to read or listen to the radio and allow my sore, stiff limbs to relax and ease off. I used to feel very guilty about doing that and beat myself up because I was often on my bed at night before most primary school-age children! However, I thought it through and consoled myself with the fact that I wasn't actually sleeping, and there's no real difference between sitting in a chair reading, etc., or lying down doing it - it's just a matter of which way you feel most comfortable. There were also tips to help sleep - the usual stuff I already knew about called 'sleep hygiene' - not having a TV in your bedroom, limiting caffeine from afternoon onwards, making sure the room is dark and not too hot, etc.

My sleep efficiency did creep up a bit, but I don't think that was really the content of the App, more the fact that it stopped me stressing about my sleeplessness a little and also provided a bit of comfort that once again I was trying to do something to tackle my situation. By the end of the six-week programme unfortunately I wasn't cured at all, but I'm still glad I did it. I felt it might help 'normal' people suffering sleeplessness, but it wasn't really able to tackle parky sleeplessness as the reasons are different. Sometimes your tremor, discomfort, or dystonia keep you awake, and some people have difficulty turning at night so wake up trying to do so. No App is going to cure those physical sleep obstacles.

I didn't notice any immediate difference from using the lightbox. I wish I'd bought one with an alarm setting function, so it actually wakes me up with its light. I reckon that would be more effective, particularly if you have a memory like mine that doesn't come alive for some time first thing in the morning, so regularly forgets to switch it on even though it's right in front of my nose.

The melatonin had an effect that was, in hindsight, as hilarious as it was hideous! It gave me the most unbelievable restless legs. I'd end up wildly kicking them around in the air and over the edge of the bed trying to get rid of that awful creeping feeling you get! I'm surprised I didn't do myself an injury or break anything.

As for the new Rasagiline tablet, thank heavens I didn't get a repeat of the horrendous side effects the patches had given me. I am still taking it but am not entirely convinced it's doing anything positive. I currently take it in the morning but am wondering whether perhaps night-time might be better, as I suspect it may be contributing to my dreadful daytime tiredness. I'll consult my online parky pals and see what they think, and when they take theirs.

26. IN HINDSIGHT

I would be really interested to know if sleep problems really are an early indication of Parkinson's Disease, as it would give me a much better idea of how far back in my life this destructive disease was starting to take hold. So far, I haven't been able to find any concrete research findings on this, just theories like virtually everything else with Parkinson's.

As they say though, 'Hindsight has 20-20 Vision'. When I think carefully over the years there are a good few things that certainly were indications of the PD to come, and others that do make me wonder whether they were related as well.

One particular day about seven years ago stands out in my mind. It was a Saturday morning and later that day I was due to be going to a rehearsal with a top-notch function band I had never played with before. I was lying in bed contemplating getting up and a couple of weird things started happening. I began to get the oddest waves of a completely strange smell sensation. I couldn't figure out what it was but somehow knew it wasn't an actual smell that existed but something happening within me. It's incredibly difficult to explain, but it wasn't pleasant, and nothing would take it away. I tried smelling some perfume, but the waves still came, underlining that the weird feeling wasn't a 'physical' smell but something to do with my brain's interpretation of my sense of smell.

I was also a little apprehensive about the rehearsal as it was new music with a new bunch of people, and I knew I had to perform well – I was to be doing a well-paid gig with them. Whilst lying there in bed every time I thought about the practice ahead, my right hand started to shake. I knew I wasn't that nervous - how weird! I've played and performed in plenty of new situations, in fact, it used to be my bread and butter, and that's never happened before.

Once I was up and showered, I went downstairs but the strange smell waves kept happening. I asked my husband and son if they could smell it, but of course, they couldn't. From then on, the weird smell thing kept happening and still does. I also became aware that my general sense of smell was deteriorating, from having had a really acute sense of smell when I was younger.

At that time, apart from my day job, I was also helping to renovate a flat. We had already done a few refurbishments and I found it a great release from normally being sat at a computer screen doing accounts. My mind got a rest and I liked the physical effort and activity the DIY jobs needed. I was still enjoying running so was pretty fit, but I noticed I was finding it more difficult to get up and down off the floor if I was doing something like painting skirting boards. Bending to pick things up also seemed to need more effort and I seemed to do it more clumsily. I put it down to old age creeping in, but there was a niggling feeling of something strange about it.

The third marked thing that came around that time too was when I was speaking to anyone about something I found quite emotive my right side would start shaking, sometimes quite violently. It was embarrassing! It didn't use to happen. Again, what was I to think?

Loss of sense of smell, sleep issues, stiffness, and tremor are of course all common confirmed Parkinson's symptoms. But other things over my life also make me wonder whether they were related.

Reasonably recently I have suffered three intense and lengthy bouts of frozen shoulder, all on my Parkinson's side. The first was a few years ago, and the other two since my PD diagnosis. The first one I put down to hand sanding a pile of doors during one of the refurbishments, but the other two just appeared. Strange though - I used to play squash every day and if anything would be likely to bring on frozen shoulder, you'd think it might be that. There is some discussion in medical circles as to whether this condition is indeed more common amongst the PD community. The anecdotal evidence I've come across in the various social media forums and support sites I follow would suggest it perhaps is.

Looking back at my life in general I would say that I've always felt I have less physical stamina than other people. Perhaps that's simply because of poor sleep but I think it's more ingrained in my make-up than that. I've never been far away from having a nap, even at a young age. I must be careful though, of blaming absolutely everything on Parkinson's, as it is possibly more likely to be my inherited Hypertrophic Cardiomyopathy that is responsible for lack of energy or stamina. Although it took fifty-odd years to find out, I was born with that heart defect. Perhaps it's nothing to do with either of them and it's actually just because I was a cat in a previous life and am programmed to love sleep!

When the real Parkinson's symptoms did start to manifest themselves more obviously, I felt like I had to wait for an age for a firm diagnosis. However, some people seem to go for an incredible number of years before their PD becomes 'official'. I've become a bit of a 'PD Spotter' since my diagnosis, I can't help it! A while back I was watching BBC News and the reporter Rory Cellan Jones was doing an article on 5G technology. During his report, you could clearly see the oh too familiar stiffness and tremor in his right arm and hand. I immediately thought, 'He's got Parkinson's'. It seems I wasn't alone. As a result of concerned people, including a neurologist, contacting the BBC he sought medical advice and a short time later announced that sure enough, he did have PD.

Parkinson's is not to be wished upon anyone, but high-profile people with it do at least help spread the word about this relatively misunderstood disease. I've already mentioned perhaps the most famous sufferer worldwide, Michael J. Fox. Here in Scotland, our great Comedian Billy Connolly's diagnosis has certainly brought Parkinson's more to the fore.

My own personal hero is the Sky Sports Darts Presenter Dave Clark. He was diagnosed in 2011 at the same age as his father was, 44 - and had to deal with the diagnosis knowing the disease had resulted in his father taking his own life because of it - he was 17 at the time. Dave even kept his diagnosis secret for two and a half years for fear of losing the TV job he loved. Doctors had told him he probably had about two to three years of live television presenting left before the Parkinson's would make it impossible to carry on. In fact, he managed nine, only making the decision to step down in early 2020. He has raised more than half a million pounds for Parkinson's UK in that time and I haven't enough words to express how inspirational I find his positivity and determination.

27. A TOUGH JOB

Hats off to anyone, like Dave Clark and Rory Cellan Jones, who hold down a job with Parkinson's Disease.

I decided to give up my broadcasting career when I found out I was expecting my son. I was freelancing at the time and my working pattern could be quite unpredictable. In the fifteen years I'd been doing it I had pretty much achieved all I really wanted, and also didn't particularly like the way the broadcast industry was heading - becoming 'cheap and cheerful' in some cases, with standards and production values dropping. I'd had the time of my life though, met people and did things I would never normally in a million years have had the chance to do, and most of all worked with some fabulous colleagues - whose talent, drive, humour, and integrity were of the best.

For the next twenty years, I joined my husband, running and growing a facilities management business. It was relentless, as I'm sure most people with their own business will agree. Especially so when my elderly parents were alive too, and it was a three-way juggle between work, our young son, and their deteriorating health.

The business gave us a very good living, which we never took for granted, and we both loved and hated it - thankfully much more loved than hated, but there were definitely plenty of stressful moments that had us tearing our hair out. It was time-intensive and both physically and mentally demanding, and we both knew at some point we'd have to call it a day. The diagnosis of my heart condition and then Parkinson's Disease brought on that day, and we decided to put our company on the market.

After eighteen months of negotiation and all the legalities that go with commercial sales, on 31st August 2018 we officially retired. It was the best and the weirdest feeling in the world! Neither of us had ever not worked all our adult lives after university.

My priority was my health. The last two and a half years had been exceptionally hard keeping my work on an even keel while my body was experiencing an increasing rollercoaster of good and less good days. Some mornings I was absolutely whacked by the time I'd showered and dressed, let alone done the day's work, and you can't say to staff 'oh I wasn't feeling great today so I haven't paid you.' There were other times when sitting at my computer for hours to meet accounts deadlines brought on agonising muscle spasms and subsequent headaches that I had no choice but to work through to get finished what had to be done. Plus, absolutely everything was taking longer and longer because of the gradual deterioration in my writing and typing with my parky hand, and things like getting sheets of paper into envelopes and poly-pockets could take half a dozen wobbly attempts.

At the same time our son was heading off to university a hundred plus miles away, and we moved from our house with many steps to one across the road with far fewer steps! 2018 was quite a year but it couldn't have all come at a better time!

I try my absolute best every day not to think about what my retirement could have been like. I had visions of running, hillwalking, cycling, swimming, driving to visit friends I'd never had time to go and see, exploring new places, playing lots more music, maybe even a bit of music teaching - and the list goes on. The reality has turned out, as you'll have guessed having got this far through the book, to be heartbreakingly different.

If I let myself think about that though, I will for certain slide into despair. There is no point, absolutely nothing to be gained and plenty to be lost by doing that - I have no choice but to focus on the things I *can* do and I am always looking for more things 'the new parky me' might do in the future. Oh I have my moments of frustration and despair - don't for one second think I don't - but thankfully they never last long.

Yes, I still cycle, swim, do neuro pilates and go to the gym but I am concentrating on increasing the repertoire of things I can do when my body is not cooperating. I've taught myself to crochet (!) and this year I raised annuals from seed rather than buying them in the garden centre. I call these tasks my 'crinkle-cut' things.

I need to think up lots more! More cats to add to the two we already have would be an excellent way of filling my time but sadly I haven't convinced my family about that. I wonder if cats could come on prescription what with pet therapy and all that?

Parkinson's is much more commonly an older person's disease so sadly but inevitably there seems to be a lack of resources for and focus on those of younger working age that have it. I recently took part in an online research project into the effects of Parkinson's on the mind, both memory, and emotion. It consisted of answering what they termed as 'real-life situation' questions and invariably they said things like, 'You are looking after your grandson for the day...', or,

'It is the third day you have had a different carer come to help you...'. Hmmm... the only qualifying criteria for participation was that you had to have had PD for more than three years - that doesn't make you old!

I was very lucky in that having our own business I had no boss (much as my husband may beg to differ!), but I dread to think how little understanding there must be out there in the workplace for employees with Parkinson's.

As a former boss myself I would have, in earlier years, been totally uninformed as to how it would affect a member of staff and how they could be supported. I, like most, barely knew what Parkinson's was. Then when I found myself in the position of having to work with PD I really could have done with support on the practical difficulties of such things as struggling to write and type, take telephone messages, etc. I was able to teach myself to write with my left hand, but I know from the responses I've had to my blog post on it, that many aren't. Where is the help for them? Perhaps that will be my next mission...

28. OUR WEIRD WORLD

2020 started innocently and on quite a high with my successful appointment with the New-Neurologist! Little did we all realise what was ahead of us with the deadly Covid 19 pandemic. I had hoped I'd hear fairly quickly from him with a date for my next appointment in six months time as promised, but nothing came. Then as the crisis heightened and medical staff were re-deployed on to the 'Covid frontline' I knew nothing more would happen any time soon.

When I used to run regularly, I was lucky and seemed to rarely have any injuries, but strangely with Parkinson's injuries were increasingly starting to appear out of nowhere. In summer 2019 I got a really bad dose of plantar fasciitis (basically a horrendously sore foot). I have no idea how - one day it was fine, the next day it was super painful and I was hurpling around for ages. After that, it was a pain that started where my leg joins on to my body at the front, whatever you call that bit, (the bit that's where the hinge is on an Action Man's leg – or maybe Barbie Doll in my case? Actually, I think I'm more Action Man than Barbie Doll!) going right down my thigh to the knee. I couldn't lift my leg at all to put my trousers on for ages! Again - it came out of the blue! (Don't worry, I didn't go trouserless, sitting down did the trick!)

When the new year dawned it brought with it a new pain - a belter of a sore knee. I swear I did not do anything untoward to it that might have caused it, I was just minding my own business doing my weekly pilates and going to the gym as normal, not even cycling as the winter weather was a bit too evil, it is Scotland after all! It gradually got so bad it kept me awake at nights and at times I could barely walk. I hoped it would right itself of its own accord especially as we went into lockdown. With my gym and pilates off the cards it was getting an enforced rest, but as one bit of it improved another part got worse.

It was getting ridiculous and I desperately needed my magic cure of all ills - my physios, but they were locked down too with face to face appointments banned. Catastrophe! Thankfully, I managed to reach my MSK physio by email and begged him for help. The poor man, I give him no peace. I could just imagine the rolling of his eyes, 'what's she gone and done now!' look, but his endless patience shone through once again - he really is a star. There followed an online dialogue of explanations and videos to him, exercises and advice back from him, back and forth, back and forth. When my moaning reached a new high, he advised a set of walking sticks if I could lay my hands on any, to give me a little extra support from the pain to help me keep moving. Luckily, I still had them from when I'd broken my ankle.

What ensued was erm.... interesting, the moral of the tale being that walking sticks don't work too well when you're a parky, particularly one in an OFF state! I decided a short stroll on a sunny day would be just the tonic aided by my sticks and set off confidently with the opposite stick to foot as you do. It quickly became apparent that my parky arm was not going to move the stick forward in unison with my good leg, and I ended up dragging it (the stick) half the time. Quite quickly my parky hand became sore from gripping the stick, so I started dropping it too. It ended up a cacophony of arms, legs, and sticks all over the place and I had no choice but to head for home and a re-think! I decided to re-group and repeat this time using arm crutches instead - I figured at least I had less chance of dropping them. It was marginally more successful, but I got so swamped by neighbours who'd seen me sending messages saying 'Oh no, saw you out with crutches, what's happened?' that I decided to knock the whole idea on the head!

What is it about my muscles these days that they seem to damage so easily? I came up with a theory not long after when a new Parkinson's symptom altogether started to rear its ugly head. Never a dull moment with this damn disease.

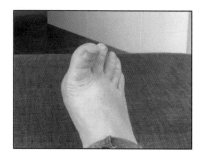 

The joy of dystonia had reached me - the involuntary movement of muscles. My big toe started curling upwards and my ankle twisting, then a little time later my index finger joined in and started curling under. If you've ever had your toes curl with cramp, it's a bit like that. My toes and foot also started moving constantly at times and I couldn't stop them. This is dystonia's sidekick dyskinesia. These are all precursors to that squirming I mentioned previously that Michael J. Fox does. They can be caused by the drugs but can also be a symptom of your OFF state - in my case I think the latter.

I got my husband to video me trying to walk during a dystonia/dyskinesia spell and it was awful, making my foot twist out with every step. My theory, therefore, is that the various aches and pains are caused by what's going on elsewhere. That weird twisting out thing must be having an impact on my opposite knee, which is perhaps why it is so damn sore! The 'Action Man' top of the leg down to knee thing is back with a vengeance too, so getting my lower half clothes on is a painful struggle again.

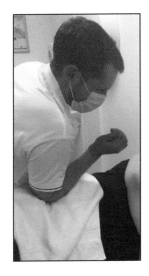

More than anything I was waiting for the 'release' of my MSK physio from lockdown. I knew he would yet again pick me up, brush me down, and set me straight, ready to fight another day – and he did.

I swear he has beyond-human capabilities - the very next day I could get my knickers on without an ounce of pain!

Hip flexor was the main culprit this time apparently. He used his evil elbow-of-torture, and gave me some exercises to do.

As for the knee, his killer thumbs saw to that. Careful, gradual strengthening in the gym, using light weights initially, he told me.

I will do these diligently. Never mess with your physio – mark my words, they have the power to inflict much pain on patients who slack with their exercises!

I tried to contact my PD nurse to ask her opinion on the arrival of my dystonia/dykinesia. She didn't reply and eventually I got a message to say she'd retired. I seem to have that effect on PD nurses, one appointment with me and they're gone forever!

Fingers crossed though, somewhere along the line in the not too distant future there will be a new Parkinson's nurse and an appointment to see New-Neurologist again too.

29. JUST ANOTHER DAY

Monday 10th August 2020

I wake up at 5am having been awake a couple of times already in the night, but that's nothing new, in fact, it was a pretty good night for me. I'm not too tired just now which looks promising - perhaps it's going to be a good day? Who knows - only time will tell.

The cats have woken up with me, so I'll go downstairs to feed them and let them out. Their eager little faces never fail to make me smile regardless of how rotten I might feel.

I dread my first cumbersome move of each day - turning round to sit on the edge of the bed for a minute or so to give my body time to acclimatise. Sometimes this parky lark can make you a bit dizzy at first, so you need to be careful, but I'm okay today.

I stand up stiffly. My right leg is sore. I guess it's been living a life of its own during the night, the muscles contracting and twisting having their own nocturnal parky party! At least they let me sleep reasonably well though - sometimes they don't. My right arm is in full-on tremor mode making my shoulder stiff and uncomfortable, so walking is awkward. I move forward clumsily and go downstairs, one step by one step, like an overgrown toddler, holding on to both bannisters. My knee hurts today - ouch! It was fine yesterday - where did that come from? The cats dance around my feet excitedly as I make my way rigidly to the kitchen.

I've been unmedicated since taking my last levodopa dose at about 5.30pm last night - I am a parky in its raw state.

I see to the cats and make myself a cup of tea to take back to bed and contemplate my day ahead. Time to work out what I'm going to be doing and decide whether I need to perform a medication juggling act to make sure I'm human rather than robot at the right times.

Hmmm, now let me think... It looks like it's going to be a quiet day (we're back in partial Covid lockdown) with just the boiler service man coming at 3.30 pm, so if I give him say, a two-hour window from 3.30 to 5.30, that means I need to take my middle dose of levodopa a bit later than usual or it might wear off too early and I really don't want to be in big-wobble when he's here. Since I've nothing I need to get done particularly early I'll perhaps leave the first dose a little later too, that way I should have a fairly stable day rather than a horrible OFF period in the middle.

I while away some time in bed with my tea listening to the news on the radio (once a journalist always a journalist!), catching up on emails and social media, and thinking through the other things I'd like to get done today like washing my car, some pilates perhaps and going on a bike ride. I'd normally take my first dose of levodopa about 8.30am but I'll leave it till 9.30 to fit in with the boiler/medication plan. That means I'll have to have my breakfast by 8.30 or after 10.30, so there's not a protein clash.

I could get up and have a shower, but quite honestly, it's too much effort when I'm still in my pre-medicated state - so I'm forced into a slow parky morning waiting for it to take effect. How different things are from the old days of jumping out of bed at 6, getting showered, breakfasted, and ready in no time to dash to work! It'll be the back of ten o'clock before my medication really kicks in today and I can move well enough to start doing anything useful.

By mid-morning, my meds are working, and I was right - it looks like it is going to be a pretty good parky day. Pity I didn't have more planned, typical! It's endlessly annoying that my days are so unpredictable and it's so difficult to plan anything. Unfortunately, the weather isn't on my side for the outdoor things I'd hoped to do, so I take the time to get some cleaning done instead. My limbs are moving well. Woohoo!

I am aiming to hold off taking my next dose of levodopa till about 2pm so it's good right through till boiler completion time about 5.30pm, but by 1.15pm I'm starting to feel I'm going 'OFF'. My tremor is coming back, I'm stiffening up and everything is becoming an effort again. Thank goodness I'm retired and can just go and sit down. I plan a carbohydrate-based lunch as it's a bit too close to my next lot of tablets to eat much protein.

It's 3pm, the heating engineer will be here soon and I'm 'ON' - so far so good with the medicine juggle... except I could fall asleep in a second given half a chance. I'll do my best to look alert when he arrives! If he's quick I might even be able to sneak in a quick forty winks before my evening meal. That would be nice.

As it turned out I got my nap, but only because the darned man didn't turn up - aaaargh! I wasn't quite spot on with the timings of my medication and only just made it to 5.30pm without too much 'OFF' setting in, but by 5.50pm I was totally 'OFF'. I took another tablet and then waited for it to get into my system and do its thing before eating my meal or it would be too difficult to operate cutlery and I wouldn't enjoy my food.

Once I've eaten, unless I have something specific I must do, I generally avoid arranging anything for the evening. I've always been a morning person rather than an evening one at the best of times, but these days I'm often absolutely whacked by then and all I want to do is rest my weary body. I hate letting people down and changing arrangements, so I'd rather not make them in the first place. It also means a total re-timing of my tablets to stretch them out to night-time - which puts me completely to pot!

I am not a TV watcher at all, in fact, I could happily not have one, so I generally occupy my evenings doing things like organising any home improvements or repairs, boring household admin like bank stuff or insurance, etc., reading or researching things that interest me, and writing. My brain never stops - sometimes I really wish it would!

The dystonia and dyskinesia in my foot are bad right now. It's 7.30pm - my big toe is curling and when it isn't my toes and foot won't stop moving. It might be hard getting to sleep later if it doesn't calm down. I'll try pinning it under my other foot to keep it still but that doesn't usually work for long.

It's 9.15pm and I'm in bed. Thankfully, I got my teeth brushed before my meds wore off completely - it's so much easier and less messy!

9.45pm and they're totally OFF now so that's me back to my raw state until I get back on the rollercoaster tomorrow morning. My hand tremor is full-on, my upper arm uncomfortable and stiff, and as a surprise treat tonight, unusually my lower leg is tremoring a little too. At least the dystonia and dyskinesia are subsiding though, so that's something.

I find it quite difficult to read when I'm tremoring a lot so either Radio 4, the BBC World Service, or an audiobook will see me off to sleep. Whether I will actually sleep and for how long is another matter...

It's 10.25pm - and that was an ordinary Parkinson's day for ordinary me. I guess things could be a whole lot worse, and at some point, they will be, so I cherish what I can do, and I'll take one-by-one each new day and the challenges it brings.

I switch off the light on the first five years of my Parkinson's Disease journey.

30. THE MOST PRECIOUS THING

I was going to call this the Epilogue but it's not, it's really the Prologue - as every moment that passes is a new part of the life I love and am so incredibly grateful for. I'll soon be 56 years-old and Parkinson's has taught me not to take the gift of time for granted.

Every day I remind myself that the best things in life are free so I'll embrace them and enjoy them - the wind in my hair, the sun on my face, the birdsong in my early morning waking hours, and most of all the special people I have in my life, and the last five years have taught me who those really are. I intend to do everything I can to see 66, 76, and maybe even 86 years of age with them.

I am blessed to have had a safe, secure, and loving childhood with parents I adored and respected. They gave me the wherewithal to tackle life's challenges, be my own person, and uphold the values they believed in and instilled in me. I owe it to them to do that. I miss them more than words can say but I am thankful they know nothing of the Parkinson's path I find myself on. It would have broken their hearts.

I will follow in their footsteps and pass on the unconditional love they gave me to the most precious thing I possess, my son. My heart is his, now and forever.

Parkinson's is my demon but I'm not fighting it I'm negotiating with it, and all the time we are finding new ways to live life together.

I still have so much to do and to give, and if the time comes when I physically can't then hopefully mentally I still can instead. But the day I feel I am no longer able to give and just take, is the day I will call it the end, I will not wait for it to call my end.

Just Wobbling Along

Printed in Great Britain
by Amazon